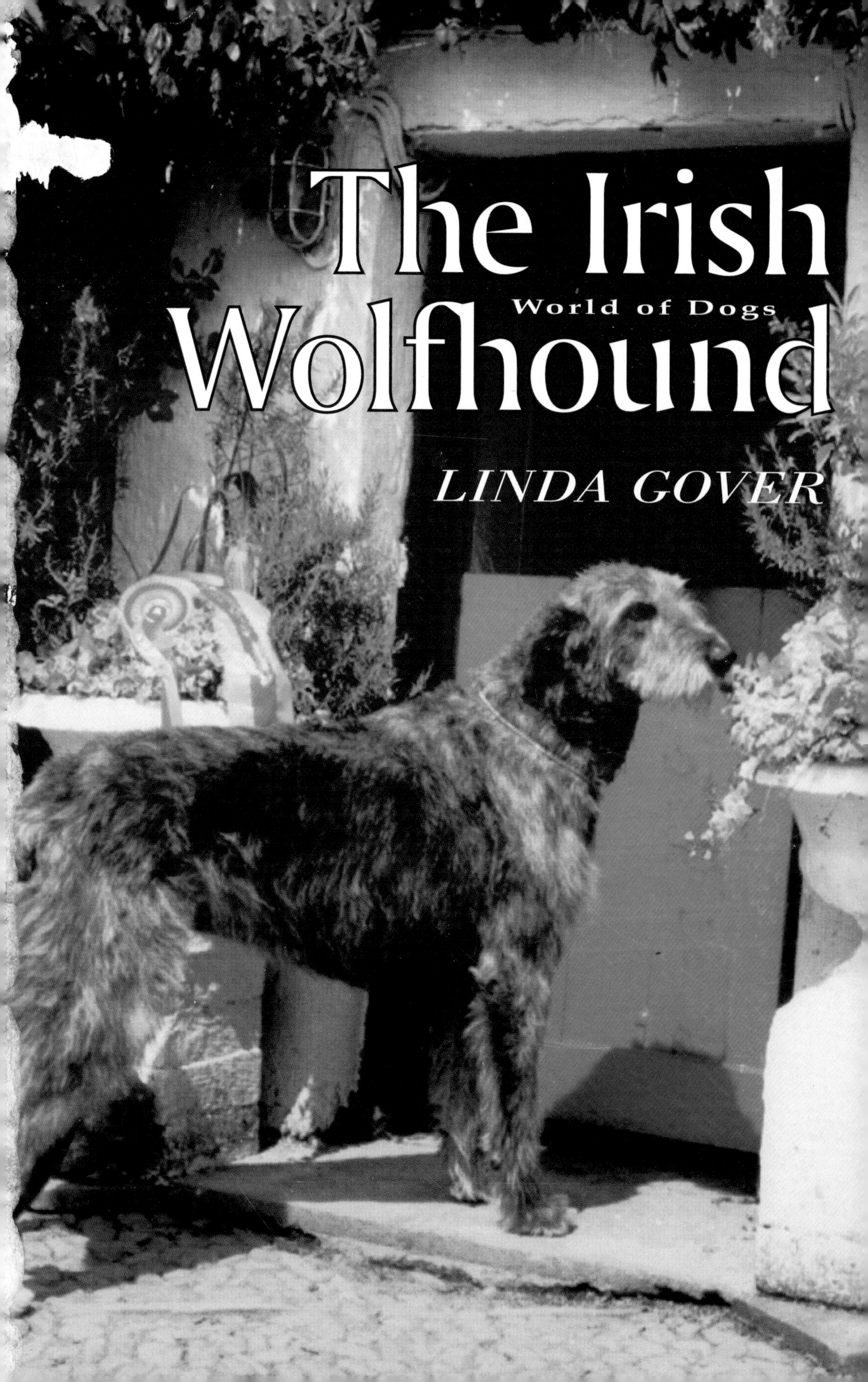
The Irish Wolfhound
World of Dogs
LINDA GOVER

t.f.h.
KINGDOM

CONTENTS

Front cover: Two of the author's champions: Ch Owenmore Kestrel and Ch Owenmore Kingfisher.
Title page: Ch Owenmore Kittiwake.
Contents page: Ch Owenmore Ciara. Photo: Robert Smith

The author exercising Owenmore hounds.

When first asked to write a book about the breed I love and admire and that for 20 years has shared my life my instinctive reaction was to decline. The brief seemed almost impossible: *cover all aspects and be interesting and informative to all readers, from those just contemplating buying an Irish Wolfhound to those who have had them for many years...* Were it not for persistent gentle bullying from a husband whose unshakable faith in my abilities is sometimes overwhelming, coupled with great encouragement from my friends in this and other breeds, this book would not have been written.

I have tried to give, as simply as possible, a broad picture of life with the Irish Wolfhound, based on my experiences, hoping in particular to help newer owners better understand the special needs of these hounds and some of the small problems that may arise, so that the love and companionship of this most aristocratic and gentle sighthound can be enjoyed to the full. No doubt many experienced owners will not agree with some of my ideas but, since controversy is the lifeblood of the dog world and seldom is any single concept indisputably right or wrong, this must be good if only in providing food for thought.

I make no apology for writing this book with an Irish bias. The Wolfhound is a magnificent and historically important native breed of which Ireland is justifiably proud. Throughout the book, the letters 'Ch' before a hound's name indicates an Irish Champion: all other champions are qualified (GB Ch, US Ch, Aus Ch and so on).

I should like to thank Elizabeth Murphy, President of the Irish Wolfhound Club of Ireland, for permission to reprint the *Standard of Excellence* and for photographs of her own and other people's hounds.

I hope the ancillary chapters and articles written by such knowledgeable breed enthusiasts will provide an interesting overall view of the world of Irish Wolfhounds. In this respect, I especially wish to make known that everyone who so kindly contributed to this volume did so in good faith and trust in my integrity, but with no foreknowledge of my own text, so must not be construed or adjudged as necessarily agreeing with me.

I am particularly grateful to Michelle Bedford of the Carrigrohan affix who so carefully read, analysed and criticised each fledgling chapter. Her enquiring mind and search for knowledge alerted me to points which might otherwise have been overlooked. Special thanks too to George Kinsella MVB, MA, MRCVS for taking time from his busy practice to write about homeopathy and to proof read and check my facts in the health and veterinary chapter.

I am indebted to Francis McEvoy of Australia and Jane Usmar of New Zealand for taking time to write reports on the state of the breed in the Antipodes. The chapters on lure coursing and obedience reflect respectively the expertise and enthusiasm of John R Davies of the United States of America and Connie Banks of Canada, without whose help these subjects probably would not have been covered. Thanks also to Mr W Hasselbrink, Secretary of the Federation of European Irish WolfhoundClubs (EIWC), for permission to give information about the newly-formed Federation.

A special 'thank you' must go to Tony Killykeen-Doyle for information about past kennels and his generosity in allowing me to go through his collection of photographs.

I am indebted to so many people who entrusted me with precious photographs that I prefer not to name individuals in case I inadvertently forget someone. Be assured that I am no less grateful!

My thanks also go to TFH/Kingdom Books for inviting me to write this book – an exercise I have thoroughly enjoyed.

Finally, before boring you into reading no further, my very sincere thanks for being curious enough to pick up and open this book, in which I trust you will find something to interest, amuse or annoy. May you have as much joy and pleasure in sharing your life with Irish Wolfhounds as I do. They truly are a unique and very special breed.

Linda Gover

CHAPTER ONE

The O'Mahony, Knight of Kerry, with Granua.
Courtesy of A Killykeen-Doyle.

HISTORY AND REVIVAL OF THE IRISH WOLFHOUND

Early history

There is evidence that hunting dogs resembling Irish Wolfdogs were in Greece and Cyprus around 1400 BC, and very early Greek and Roman authors describe Celtic dogs and Gallic hounds as suited to and swift in the chase, as well as being used on the battlefield. As early as the second century AD a Greek writer, Flavius Arrianus, gave an in-depth description of the Celtic Greyhound with a list of points and said it could be smooth- or rough-coated. He went on to praise its gentle temperament and need for human companionship as well as describing its hunting methods in his manual on coursing. He himself had one such hound, which shared his bed and his table.

In the fourth century, some time before 391 AD, the Roman Consul Quintus Aurelius Symmachus wrote to his brother Flavianus, thanking him for his gift of seven Irish hounds which had been shown for the first time in Rome. They had caused a great stir because of their size, the inhabitants thinking they must have been brought there in iron cages. These were probably Irish Wolfdogs, as the Romans at that time were well used to English Mastiffs. The fact that seven hounds were given also indicates that they came from Ireland, as this was the accepted number for a present of horses or dogs from one Irish notability to another. Thus we have proof that for many centuries great Celtic hunting hounds of impressive size and speed have been bred and shipped from Ireland as highly-prized gifts to dignitaries of other lands.

History and legend in Ireland

The earliest history of the breed in Ireland was passed on in the vernacular through the myths, legends and sagas, and it is from these that we learn of the existence, form and characteristics of the ancient Irish hunting hounds. It seems that from time immemorial the people of Ireland loved everything connected with the chase, and hounds have always taken a prominent place in the life of the country. Held to be more ancient even than the Gods, the Fomors were a hideous and ferocious race who came from the sea. When they met with warriors at the battle of Moytura they asked: 'Whence do you come?' 'From Ireland,' was the answer. The Fomorians then asked: 'Have you hounds with you?' They had, so a dog-race was run and the Irish hounds proved the faster.

Mythology also tells many stories of the *Tuatha dé Danann* (Tribe of the Goddess Danu), a tall and beautiful family of divinities who lived and hunted with their great hounds around the *Brun na Boinn* (Boyne Valley), which is dominated by the megalithic tomb of Newgrange, dated around 3200 BC. These peoples were Gaels, the earliest of the Celtic races who settled here.

Felixstowe Regan.
Courtesy of A Killykeen-Doyle.

Great were their deeds, their passions and their sports:
With clay and stone
They piled on strath and shore those mystic forts,
Not yet o'erthrown;
On cairn-crowned hills they held their council-courts;
While youths alone,
With giant dogs, explored the elk resorts,
And brought them down.

Since the first century AD, the history of the breed in Ireland has been well documented. This was the time of young Setanta who, when attacked by it, killed the ferocious watchdog that guarded the property of the chief smith, Culann. Overcome with remorse for slaying this much-valued animal, Setanta offered to take the place of the hound until he could train another to equal ability, and from then on he was known as *Cu-Chulainn* (the Hound of Culann).

Cu-Chulainn was a nephew of King Conchubar and his own favourite hound was called Luath, signifying speed. Cu-Chulainn seems to have been a semi-divinity in that he had exceptional strength and super-human powers and his fearless and heroic deeds became legendary. He it was who fought long, hard and sometimes single-handed in the great war described in the epic *Táin Bó Chuailgné* (the Cattle Raid of Cooley), which tells the story of Queen Mebd and the Brown Bull of Ulster. Reports show that hounds were frequently taken into battle, and on one battlefield Cu-Chulainn rages: *In equal case were hounds, horses and men, slain lying in heaps on the ground.* In his 27th year the great warrior was mortally wounded but tied himself to a pillar-stone so that he might die on his feet. His head was cut off and presented to Queen Mebd.

When the sons of Uisnech were exiled by King Conor, in their flight from Ulster into Scotland they took with them 150 greyhounds as well as 150 warriors and 150 serving-men.

Another tale tells how the children of Lir, finding their father's residence *Sídh Fionnachaidh* (Hill of the White Field) deserted, cried and sang: *A wonder to me in this place, without a dwelling... it is bitterness to my heart – without hounds, without packs of them.*

The sons of Tuirenn had to fight a fierce battle and take the King of Iruaide prisoner before they could seize his prized hound-whelp, before whose beauty all the beasts of the world fell prostrate to pay homage.

This was the ancient greyhound
Which belonged to Lug of the Mantles,
To whom the sons of Tuirenn gave it;
That hound of mightiest deeds,
Which was irresistible in hardness of fight,
Was better than any wealth whatever
A thunderbolt every night...

The third or fourth century was the time of the great hunter and warrior Finn mac Coul. Of more lowly birth than Cu-Chulainn, he was chief of King Cormac's household and master of his hounds. Three hundred of the hounds are named in the many verses written by Finn's son, the poet Oisin, who tells of the exploits of his father and the Fenians. All the hounds were much loved and admired for their hunting ability, but Bran (a bitch) is said to have been Finn's favourite and the one who shared her master's bed. He would let no harm befall her, and her wisdom, strength, speed and prowess caused much to be written in her praise and places to be named after her. She gave her name to Lough Bran when she caused a lake to spring up through pawing up the earth in fury because an enchanted doe she was pursuing vanished when overtaken by her. She could catch wild geese in flight and was the only hound who had ever hunted the magical wild boar of Ben Gulbein. Bran had a daughter, a black bitch who became the pride of the Fenians and was thought to have inherited some of her mother's magical powers. The first record of dog-stealing is when one of Finn's servants ran off to Britonland with three hounds, Bran, Sceolaing and Adnuall, who were only recovered after a hard fight. Sadly, it was Finn himself who accidentally killed Bran as she was in full flight after another enchanted doe, although it is said that she and Sceolaing have

Margaret Harrison (centre) with GB Ch Sanctuary Rory of Kihone and progeny.
Courtesy of A Killykeen-Doyle.

never really died as they were transformed by a witch into the mountain *Sliabh da Chon* (the Mountain of the Two Hounds) in Fermanagh.

There are many stories of the great hunts and fights of the Fenians and their hounds. During one such hunt near Loch Bô a pirate's greyhound, described as a *shag-haired dog of dirty grey,* is slipped at Oisin's cousin, Cáilte, but killed by him. We are told that Cáilte and his companions were tall men accompanied by huge Wolfdogs. Oisin's own two favourite hounds were Feruaine and Adhnuall, who accompanied him to the Land of the Young to which he had been cajoled by the Fairy Queen with the promise of 'a hundred keen and eager hounds'. When he returned to this world all his old friends were gone and St Patrick was preaching Christianity, to which Oisin was converted, asking to take his hounds with him into Paradise. There are several stories showing St Patrick's affinity with the Wolfdogs and innumerable other tales involving the great hounds.

From ninth century AD

It seems that when the Danes came to invade Ireland they were very impressd with the huge dogs, and many stories of Irish dogs have entered Scandinavian folklore. In the ninth or tenth century the *Saga of Burnt Njal* records Olaf, a Norwegian, son of an Irish princess, telling his friend Gunnar: *I will give thee a hound that was given to me in Ireland; he is big, and no worse than a stout man. Besides it is part of his nature that he has a man's wit, and he will bay at every man he knows to be thy foe, but never at thy friends. He can see, too, in any man's face whether he means thee well or ill, and he will lay down his life to be true to thee.*

As time goes on more and more written references to the great Wolfdogs are found, and early Christian art depicts them in books and on shrines and crosses. The *Book of Kells* shows two Greyhounds, and hounds also adorn the Shrine of the Abbot of Clonmacnoise and the Cross of St Patrick and St Columba situated in Kells. They became highly desirable commodities and irresistible bribes for statesmen and important dignitaries. Kings and noblemen from other countries increasingly sent to Ireland for them.

In 1014 the Dalcassian soldiers at Clontarf are compared to the terrible, nimble Wolfdogs of Ireland for strength and courage, and at about this time the ancient Laws of Wales put a much higher price on the Wolfdog or Irish dog than any other greyhound or even workhorse.

King John of England, in about 1210, presented an Irish hound to Llewellyn, a Prince of Wales. The poet The Hon W R Spencer immortalised this hound, Gelert, in a wonderful and moving poem relating the story of how he killed a great wolf and saved his master's child. From this come those often-quoted lines so descriptive of the temperament of a Wolfhound:

The flower of all his race,
So true, so brave – a lamb at home,
A lion in the chase.

In his *Historie of Ireland*, completed in 1571, Blessed Edmund Campion gives a description of the hounds used for hunting the wolves on the Dublin and Wicklow mountains. He says: *They* [the Irish] *are not without wolves and greyhounds to hunt them, bigger of bone and limb than a colt.* Also from this time there is much written evidence of these hounds frequently being sent as gifts to important and noble personages of many European countries, as well as requests being received for them. Henry VIII wrote to Ireland for some and Shane O'Neill sent a brace to Queen Elizabeth I.

Tales of their prowess as swift and fearless hunters yet of a gentle disposition with their masters and other humans made them much sought after in many countries where wolves, wild boar and other game abounded. Hunting was very fashionable and popular amongst the upper classes. The King of Denmark and the Great Mogul bought every one they could get, the Emperor Jehangir asked for some to be sent, the Papal Nuncio was presented with one, and Cardinal Richelieu received one in exchange for a gold medal he had bestowed on Cardinal Ussher. Kings of Sweden and Poland received gifts of the great Irish hounds as did the Shah of Persia. Numbers became so depleted that, in Kilkenny on 27 April 1652, a declaration against transporting Wolfdogs was published by Cromwell to ensure that sufficient numbers remained to control the wolf population.

References to the Irish Wolfdog in the 1700s tell of of its great size, strength and greyhound shape as well as its scarcity. Writing in 1790, Bewick described it as the largest and most beautiful of the dog kind; about 91.5cm (36in) high, generally of a white or cinnamon colour, somewhat like a greyhound but more robust. He said their aspect was mild, disposition peaceful, and strength so great that in combat the mastiff or bulldog was far from being equal to them, and goes on: *They mostly seize their antagonists by the back and shake them to death which their great strength enables them to do.* He also declares them to be extremely rare.

The last wolf in Ireland is thought to have been killed at Myshall, Co Carlow in 1786 by a pack of Wolfdogs kept by a Mr Watson of Ballydarton. The remaining hounds, in the hands of a few families who were mainly descendants of the old Irish chieftains, were now symbols of status rather than hunters and, by the end of the century, they were said to be the last of their race.

The revival

As you follow the story of the revival of this breed, it is important to keep in mind that, in very early times, many countries had indigenous hounds resembling greyhounds in body shape but differing according to climate and hunting habitat. Several of these ancient foreign hunting breeds are thought to have evolved from inter-breeding the native dogs with the great Wolfdogs from Ireland, which passed on many of their characteristics. One must also take into account that breeds referred to historically were not necessarily of the same shape and form as those seen today.

The great similarity in type between the Irish Wolfhound and the Scottish Deerhound has always provoked controversy as to whether they were one and the same breed, merely developed along slightly differing lines to optimise ability to hunt indigenous game. Equally controversial has been the question of whether

THE IRISH PENNY JOURNAL.

NUMBER 45. SATURDAY, MAY 8, 1841. VOLUME I.

THE IRISH WOLF-DOG.

The greyhound! the great hound! the graceful of limb!
Rough fellow! tall fellow! swift fellow, and slim!
Let them sound through the earth, let them sail o'er the sea,
They will light on none other more ancient than thee!

OLD MS.

No individual of the canine race has attained an equal amount of fame, or excited an equal degree of attention through Europe, not merely in the days of his acknowledged existence amongst our dogs of chase, but even now, that he is considered to be extinct, with that once possessed by the superb creature whose picture adorns our title-page, and an account of whom forms the subject of the present article. Public opinion has long been divided respecting the precise appearance and form of this majestic animal, and so many different ideas have been conceived of him, that many persons have been induced to come to the conclusion that no particular breed of dogs was ever kept for wolf-hunting in this country, but that the appellation of "wolf-dog" was bestowed upon any dog swift enough to overtake and powerful enough to contend with and overcome that formidable animal. There are those who hold this opinion, and there are likewise those who hold that while a particular breed was used, it was a sort of heavy mastiff-like dog, now extinct. It is the object of the present paper to show that not only did Ireland possess a peculiar race of dogs exclusively devoted to wolf-hunting, but that those dogs, instead of being of the mastiff kind, resembled the greyhound in form; and instead of being extinct, are still to be met with, although we are compelled to acknowledge that they are very scarce. I myself was once in very gross error respecting this dog, for I like many others conceived him to have been a mastiff, and implicitly believed that the dogs of Lord Altamont, described in the 3d vol. of the Linnæan Transactions by Mr Lambert, were the sole surviving representatives of the Irish wolf-dog. An able and talented paper, read by Mr A. Haffield of this city, about a year ago, before the Dublin Natural History Society, served to stagger me in my belief, and subsequent careful inquiry and research have completed my conversion. I proceed to lay before my readers the

The Irish Penny Journal, showing a picture of the *Irish Wolf-dog.*

Photograph of Captain Graham standing beside his model of the ideal Irish Wolfhound.

they were smooth- or rough-coated. Father Hogan, in his book *The Irish Wolfdog*, lists reference to both coats as well as a variety of colouring. History shows that the Irish frequently went to Scotland with their hounds for hunting, although the Scots are not chronicled as crossing to Ireland with hounds. In 1521 John Major, a Scottish historian says: *It is certain that we drew our origin from the Irish.* This colonisation is also stated in Volume 1 of Hill Burton's *History of Scotland*. It can therefore be assumed that the two breeds share Irish progenitors.

Old Donagh: a painting from a Phyllis Gardner woodcut.
Courtesy of A Killykeen-Doyle.

Archibald Hamilton Rowan (1757–1834) is said to have owned the very last of the race of true Irish Wolfdogs, and many present-day Wolfhounds can be traced back to his Bran. Mr Carter of Loughlinstown strove to carry on the line from Bran and gave stock to H D Richardson, who drew attention to the near-extinction of the old breed and re-awakened interest in its revival largely through an article he wrote in *The Irish Penny Journal* of May 1841. He wrote: *Many assert the Irish Wolfdog to be no longer in existence. I hold that he and the Highland Deerhound are one and the same...* He offers proof of this, adding: *Even Glengarry, whose dogs were once so famous, has not one genuine specimen left... Why will not some of our Irish gentlemen and sportsmen turn their attention to this splendid breed of dogs, and seek to prevent, 'ere it is too late, its total extirpation.*

In 1846, in his book *The Dog: Its Origin, Natural History and Varieties*, Richardson wrote in greater depth about the Irish Wolfdog and, although he is seldom given recognition for the work he did in instigating the breed revival, his thoughts and ideas greatly influenced Captain Graham. Richardson began by mating hounds he had from Mr Carter with the somewhat heavy boned, tall Deerhounds favoured by Glengarry (who was working to re-establish these rather than the lighter, smaller strain), and it is thought that he also outcrossed to a Pyrenean, which explains why double dewclaws appear very occasionally in present-day hounds. Also actively breeding at this time, Major Garnier is known to have used a Great Dane with a Wolfdog bitch to add bone and size. Merlin, one of the progeny, said to have stood 84cm (33in) tall and weighed 68.1kg (150lb), was particularly admired and showed absolutely nothing of the Dane type.

Another gentleman anxious to preserve and restore the breed who had hounds from Richardson was Sir John Power of Kilfane, who worked closely with Mr Whyte Baker of Ballytobin Castle in breeding towards the old type. By reinforcing their own much-bred-into hounds with Glengarry stock, each built up a kennel of superb hounds, one of the best from Ballytobin being Old Donagh (see page 15), a bitch of good type who was to prove of the utmost importance to the breed. Mr O'Mahony of Dromore also worked to build up, from Kilfane stock, a slightly different line which traced directly to Hamilton Rowan's dog, Bran. He is said to have used no outcrosses.

Also around this time an Englishman, Captain George Augustus Graham (see page 14), was collecting and breeding Deerhounds. Fortunately for the breed lovers of today, he turned his great knowledge and skills to trying to *recover* (his own word) from the largest of them the Wolfdog in its original form, and he is justifiably credited with saving the breed. Working at first with just the Deerhounds, believing the *old Irish hound in its purity was extinct,* he began his dedicated objective. He collected pedigrees of Deerhounds and as many of Wolfdogs as was possible in this time when accurate breeding records were seldom kept. Throughout his work he kept meticulous records and measurements of hounds he acquired and bred. In 1879 he wrote: *It has been ascertained beyond all question that there are a few specimens of the breed still in Ireland and England that have well-founded pretensions to be considered Irish Wolfhounds, though falling far short of the requisite*

Some of Mrs Shewell's Cotswold hounds.
Courtesy of A Killykeen-Doyle.

dimensions. This blood is now in my possession. These hounds were of the Kilfane and Ballytobin strains, although he never managed to procure any of the Dromore stock, nor any from Mr Carter, whose dark grey, shaggy-coated strain had been incorporated into the Kilfane hounds. There was, in Ireland, a certain amount of prejudice against Graham and his work and he was unable to obtain as many hounds of the old blood as might otherwise have been the case. As well as Old Donagh, a very good red bitch of unknown name was acquired by Graham after Mr Baker's death and much bred into.

The task was by no means easy; bitches often failed to breed, many males were cryptorchid, and whelps frequently proved delicate. Disease such as distemper was rife and accounted for many deaths.

Graham outcrossed to the Glengarry Deerhounds that were so close to the type he was working toward and later introduced some heavy Borzoi blood, using Korotai, a large and powerful black dog owned by the Duchess of Newcastle. He also used one single cross of Tibetan Wolfdog on the very best of his in-bred bitches, Tara. The resultant progeny were of very good Wolfhound type and two of the bitches, Nookoo and Vandal, were responsible for many famous hounds in the succeeding generations. These showed little of the Tibetan influence other than a rather heavy coat. Although he did not himself use a Great Dane for an outcross, Graham had breeding stock from kennels who had used them. Although the stock with which he was breeding so successfully was numerically small, it must have been prepotent, as his strains were to breed true within a few generations – a testament to his great knowledge and deep understanding of what engenders and fixes type.

In 1885 Captain Graham was instrumental in founding the Irish Wolfhound Club, and the Breed Standard of Points that he and Major Garnier had compiled in consultation with Mr Baily was adopted and accepted by The Kennel Club. Some years previously, at a show in Dublin in 1879, the first class for Irish Wolfhounds had been held. Although there was much diversity of type amongst the hounds shown, one of the objectives in exhibiting them was to establish and agree the ideal to which breeders should aspire.

More people began to take an interest in the Irish Wolfhound and its revival. Mrs Shewell began the Cotswold kennels (see pages 16–17), and in 1902 bred a magnificent wheaten-coloured dog, over 86cm (34in) tall, said by Captain Graham to be his ideal hound. This was GB Ch Cotswold who was undefeated in the show ring. GB Ch Cotswold Patricia, a brindle standing 82.5cm (32½in) was another favourite of his and beat every bitch shown against her. Thus, before his death in October 1909, Captain Graham was assured that the type and size of Irish Wolfhound he was working to establish was safe in the hands of dedicated people.

Several breeders had been continuing the work in Ireland, including The O'Mahony, Knight of Kerry (see page 6), who perpetuated his father's old Dromore line with just one infusion of Deerhound blood. From the last litter of his old bitch, Granua, Phyllis Gardner of the Coolafin kennels had a puppy whose progeny were to prove important to such as the Raikeshill kennels owned by Mrs Knox, in Yorkshire. One of the best bitches from that kennel was Ch Lady of Raikeshill (born December 1926), who was said to be 89cm (35in) tall.

One of the most important and influential kennels was founded in 1893 by Mr Everett, who left Ireland for Suffolk and whose Felixstowe hounds soon gained an international reputation for size, type and soundness. He was a colleague of Captain Graham and could be said to be his successor, and it is largely due to his efforts that the breed survived the First World War. One of his most famous hounds was GB Ch Felixtowe Kilcullen, who stood well over 94cm (37in) tall. His stock became the foundation for many great kennels, remembered and readily traced in pedigrees today. Ouborough was owned by Mr J V Rank and masterminded by one of the great dog men of all time, Bill Siggers, who bought their first hound from Everett in 1928. She was GB Ch Clodagh of Ouborough, a bitch of 91cm (36in), who died tragically before her third year from the dreaded distemper. The Brabyns kennel of Captain and Mrs Hudson started with Felixstowe hounds, as did Sulhamstead, which was to prove so influential for Mrs Florence Nagle.

After the First World War the breed flourished, mainly in the hands of wealthy owners of large kennels and their staff. Wolfhounds of proper size and good conformation and type were carefully bred by knowledgeable and caring stock people. Hounds were being exported in increasing numbers to various countries, many to top kennels in America. Among these was Sulhamstead Dan, who was to

Chulainn Dauntless: winner of Type Cup for Bitches, 1926.

become the progenitor of many of their best hounds. The breed increased in popularity and show classes were well-filled. Many hounds gained champion titles, and there was great demand amongst kennels for each other's stock and for use of stud dogs.

With the outbreak of the Second World War, Mr Everett had all his hounds put down to prevent them from falling into the wrong hands – a very sad end to such a great kennel. He retired to a nursing home and died there in 1950. Prevailing circumstances and food shortages during the war reduced the breed to a very low ebb and valuable bloodlines were lost. Some hounds returned with their owners to Ireland where a few dedicated people were able to continue breeding with very limited stock.

After the war it became imperative to find a good outcross bloodline to impart much-needed quality and soundness. It was fortunate that, in 1951, Rory of Kihone was sent by Miss McGregor as a gift from America. He produced quality progeny from all manner of bitches, greatly improving temperament, which had degenerated. US Ch Cragwood Barney O'Shea of Riverlawn also came later to pass on his great size and commanding appearance to progeny of the few litters he sired. Irish Wolfhounds were once again bred to Captain Graham's ideals of size, conformation, quality and type.

A nucleus of knowledgeable and careful breeders kept kennels of top-class hounds into the late 1970s but now, 20 years on, there is a rising tide of consternation amongst senior breeders and judges at the noticeable decline in quality, size, soundness and health of the Wolfhounds being bred in such numbers throughout the world today.

CHAPTER TWO

Miss Sheelagh Seale with four Ballykelly champions.
Courtesy of A Killykeen-Doyle.

INFLUENTIAL KENNELS

IRELAND

It is very difficult to single out particular kennels for special mention, so I have chosen those whose affixes will probably be familiar to relative newcomers to the breed and are most likely to appear in current five- or six-generation pedigrees.

During the 1950s and 1960s some very important hounds were bred here. Dr May (who took the Ballytobin affix) produced several champions and exported excellent hounds such as US Ch Patrick of Ballytobin and Ch/US Ch Sheelagh of Ballytobin and did much to help other owners and encourage responsible breeding practices. Meanwhile, Mrs Harper produced valued and influential stock under the Ballygran affix as did Mrs Tyrrell with the Dunamaise hounds. Also actively breeding at this time were Mr Tierney of the Termon affix and the well-known John Grogan of the Fionn Uisge affix; both produced good, sound hounds whose bloodlines were important additions to many pedigrees.

Ballykelly – Miss Sheelagh Seale

Undoubtedly the most important and influential of the Irish breeders, Sheelagh Seale first became associated with Wolfhounds in the 1930s and her magnificent hounds subsequently formed the basis of many famous kennels throughout the world.

Miss Seale's first hound and foundation bitch was Avoca of Coolafin, acquired from Miss Gardner's kennel. She was a line-bred granddaughter of the famous bitch Granua, who was described in the 1920s as the last pure-bred specimen of her race. Other hounds used to found the Ballykelly line came from Grevel, Chulainn, Ouborough and Raikeshill stock.

During the war years Miss Seale lived in England, struggling to keep about 10 hounds, but she bred very few litters because of the prevailing circumstances. When she eventually returned to Ireland she brought with her Artel Ballykelly Sandy (born 1943, bred by Mrs E M Fitz-Gibbon), who won his title in both England and Ireland, becoming her first international champion. Probably her most famous and influential stud dog, Int Ch McGilligan of Ballykelly (Ch Molony of Ballykelly ex Ch An Tostal of Ballykelly), was born in 1957. He is behind nearly all hounds in Ireland today. In the 1960s Ch Ballykelly O'Flynn gained his international title, and a repeat mating of Ch Diarmuid of Dunamaise to a favourite bitch, Rooney, produced Ch Ballykelly Ni Rooney. Other hounds very special to Sheelagh were Ch Ballykelly Erislannan Liam, born 1973 and one of her last, Ballykelly To Agouri Mou.

Ballykelly hounds, a great many of whom were cream or wheaten, were renowned for their great size, substance and soundness, and the success of Miss Seale's consistent and dedicated line-breeding continues to be reflected in some of the hounds from kennels based on her stock. Ballykelly champions throughout the world are too numerous to mention, and it would be an extremely difficult task to find a pedigree that does not feature a Ballykelly hound somewhere.

Ballykelly Cavin. Courtesy of A Killykeen-Doyle.
Photo: Fionnbar Callanan

Although her life was somewhat eccentric, and at times precarious, Sheelagh Seale lived for her hounds. In 1987 she was made Patron of the Irish Wolfhound Club of Ireland and, although not in the best of health, completed the arduous task of sorting out the large entry at what was to be her final appointment: judging the breed at the Irish Kennel Club Championship Show in 1988. Miss Seale died peacefully on 9 February 1992, leaving the last of the great Ballykelly hounds in the care of John and Kathleen Kelly (Nutstown).

Ch/USA Ch Sheelagh of Ballytobin.
Courtesy of A Killykeen-Doyle.

Nendrum – Miss Noreen Twyman

Born and educated in England, Miss Noreen Twyman qualified as a veterinary surgeon before coming to live and practise in Ireland, where she was to have a great influence on the development of the breed. Her connection with Wolfhounds went back to the late 1920s and a hound called Droonagh, bought as a family pet from Mr Everett, but accompanying her when she first came to work in Ireland.

Carol of Eaglescrag was acquired in 1957 from Miss Twyman's sister, Mrs Ruth Jenkins (Eaglescrag), and won both her Irish and English titles before being mated to Int Ch McGilligan of Ballykelly in 1960 to produce her first litter. From this came the very well known Int Ch Colin of Nendrum, who had a spectacular show career. Carol's second litter, to GB Ch Sulhamstead Max, also produced champions in Corrie and Connel as well as the famous GB Ch Eaglescrag Clonroe of Nendrum (see page 24). These hounds all played an important part in the improvement and development of the breed, as did the progeny of a later litter from Corrie by GB Ch Sanctuary Brave Knight, in particular Eaglescrag Alice of Nendrum, a wonderful brood bitch influential in the Eaglescrag kennels.

As a vet and successful breeder and trainer of coursing greyhounds, Miss Twyman demanded soundness and balance in a hound, disliking exaggerations and lack of quality. She bred seldom, but was an acknowledged breed expert, much sought after as a judge for her candid and honest opinions. The Irish Wolfhound Club of Ireland was most fortunate in having her as President from 1971 until her death at home in Waterford on 18 December 1984.

GB Ch Eaglescrag Clonroe of Nendrum.

Killykeen – Anthony Killykeen-Doyle

Although 1954 marks the year Tony was given his first Wolfhound, his family's close association with them goes back many years. His great-grandmother was a daughter of Captain Hugh Richardson who did much for the breed in the 1840s, while his grandmother, Catherine Fitzpatrick-Richardson-Smith, continued to breed what she referred to as *Irish Wolfdogs*.

Tony was fortunate in having many of the breed's leading authorities of the time as peers and mentors: Delphis Gardner (Coolafin), Mrs Nagle (Sulhamstead), Miss Harrison (Sanctuary), Sheelagh Seale and, when he was sent to America to learn more, Mrs Groverman Ellis (Killybracken). He bred his first litter in 1959, mating the bitch Ballykelly Kilkenny of Killykeen to Finnigan of Ballykelly. Kilkenny's second litter was to Ch Diarmuid of Dunamaise. Both matings produced quality, sound, typical puppies, some going abroad to found new kennels. Later, Killykeen Roisin of Woodenbridge was a great favourite. A daughter of Ch Connel of Nendrum, she produced several champions and her influence is still strong in the Killykeen kennels today.

Having been absent from the show ring for some years, Tony made a successful return in the late 1980s with Killykeen Mars, an exciting young dog who fortunately left important and influential progeny before his accidental death. Mars' beautiful daughter Jermyma (see page 47), mated to Ch Edeyrn Henri of Killykeen (who traces back to Killykeen stock, and had a Best in Show (BIS) win en route to his title), produced excellent progeny, including Belg Ch Killykeen Spellbound, Ch Killykeen Wolfwitch who was top winning Wolfhound in 1991, and

Ch Killykeen McGilligan. Killykeen Max (litter brother to McGilligan) was seldom shown, but sired Ch Killykeen Destiny, who had four Hound Group wins, and the well-known litter of Owenmore champions which included Tony's Ch Owenmore Kittiwake, multiple Group winner, three times BIS winner and top winning bitch 1994. Killykeen Max has also sired top American and Canadian lure coursing, obedience and show champions.

Tony Killykeen-Doyle is much in demand on the continent as a judge of hounds and terriers. He is an acknowledged expert in the history and development of Irish Wolfhounds and his own are invariably tall, substantial, with correct coats and very sound – a long-lived and old-fashioned type of true hunting ability.

From the left: Killykeen Molly, Mark and Matthew.

Carrokeel – Miss Elizabeth Murphy

After some research, and with her father's help and advice, Miss Elizabeth Murphy came into Wolfhounds in the 1960s. She was determined to breed for improvement and consistency of type, to disprove reports from abroad that Irish-bred Wolfhounds were of poor quality and not properly bred.

Her first hounds came from the Ballykelly kennels and, in 1968, Ballykelly Sile of Carrokeel won her Irish title. She went on to produce champion progeny herself when mated to Ch Connel of Nendrum. Having let all Sile's puppies go, Betty was fortunate in being able to buy back a bitch, Carrokeel Maeve, who was mated to Nial of Dunamaise to produce the beautiful Ch Carrokeel Cara, several times winner of the Height and Soundness Cup and Best in Show (BIS) winner of the 1974 Breed Championship show. When Elsie James was going out of Wolfhounds, Betty bought in Boroughbury Justice and his sister Jolly, both of whom did well in the show ring, gaining their titles. Many breeders felt an infusion of English blood was needed, so Ch Boroughbury Justice was extensively used at stud, leaving a profound effect on the breed today.

Although she has not been breeding or showing for some years now, Betty has undoubtedly succeeded in her initial aims, with Carrokeel hounds well represented by many winning progeny and a high proportion of champions in many countries. As President of the Irish Wolfhound Club of Ireland, a Director of the Irish Kennel Club with especial interest in all Irish native breeds, and with many judging appointments to fulfil, she is kept extremely busy. Fortunately she has found time to write and publish valuable breed books, a constant source of information and reference. She is also President of the Federation of European Irish Wolfhound Clubs.

Nutstown – John and Kathleen Kelly

Having had greyhounds for some years, it was somewhat by accident in 1960 that John and Kathleen became involved with Wolfhounds when Dr May (Ballytobin) asked them to look after one for him. This was Bernie of Termon, a beautiful big bitch of Ballykelly parents. She obviously made a great impression on them since Wolfhounds have been an intrinsic part of their lives ever since.

When Dr May mated this bitch with Ch Connel of Nendrum both bitch puppies were sold, but John was later able to buy one of them: Malatown Lady. Having mated her with Ch Boroughbury Justice, he retained the lovely bitch Nutstown Queen who, in 1977, became the Kellys' first home-bred champion and was greatly influential in the future success of the kennel. Mated to Ballykelly Errislannan Liam she produced Int Ch Nutstown King, Top Winning Wolfhound in Ireland and England in 1980 and in Ireland again in 1981. He had an outstanding show career, including many wins as a Veteran, and sired many winning progeny, including Int Ch Carrokeel Sir Connel of Nutstown, Top Winning Wolfhound in 1982 with four BIS wins and many BOBs in addition to his English title (see page 28). Another son, Ch Kracken Kaiser, was also prominent in the show ring and Top Winning Wolfhound in 1983.

Carrokeel Elvin of Bearna Bui.
Photo: E C Murphy

A repeat mating of Ch Nutstown Queen with Lleigus resulted in the birth in 1979 of Sara of Nutstown, who quickly gained her Irish title but possibly gained greater fame, when mated to Kaiser, as the dam of brilliantly successful Ch Chieftain of Nutstown, notable for taking BIS at Kilkenny All-Breeds Championship Show when only six-and-a-half months old and for being the youngest-ever male Irish Wolfhound to gain his title, at just nineteen months. He was also the Irish Wolfhound Annual Champion (top points winner) for three successive years: 1986, 1987 and 1988. Ch Sara's daughter by Int Ch Carrokeel Coillte Merlin, Sorcha of Nutstown, gained her Irish title within twelve months and, with Chieftain, won many Brace classes, including that at The English Irish Wolfhound Club Championship Show.

One of John's favourite dogs is Int Ch Capitan of Shantamon, multiple Group and BIS winner and Annual Champion in 1994 and 1995. He was also named Pedigree Chum Top Sire for 1995, and a son of his, Saringas Mr Micawber, was Top Winning Puppy in Great Britain.

Although possibly best known for top-class males, John and Kathleen's Nutstown kennels have never been short of excellent bitches to carry on their bloodline. The most recent of these is Ch Blossom of Nutstown (granddaughter to

Ch Sara of Nutstown), a beautifully-made bitch of great type and quality. She was deservedly Top Winning Bitch in 1995 with Group wins, one BIS and a Reserve BIS.

With exciting younger stock such as Rosemary of Nutstown and two of Int Ch Capitan of Shantamon's sons, Fingal and Ch McGilligan, already winning well the continued success of this kennel is assured.

John and Kathleen Kelly both serve on the Irish Wolfhound Club Committee and various show committees and work tirelessly promoting the health and welfare of the breed. The distinctive Nutstown-bred champions and show winners throughout the world are too numerous to mention; all have the reputation for being very sound and healthy with excellent temperaments and are much in demand.

Ir Ch Nutstown Queen, Int Ch Nutstown King and Int Ch Carrokeel Sir Connel of Nutstown.

Gulliagh – Timothy and Marion Finney

At Gulliagh Farm in rural North Co Dublin, Timothy and Marion Finney's Gulliagh kennel overlooks the Irish Sea and the distant Mourne Mountains. Normally, between five and ten Irish Wolfhounds run together in the acreage around the house, and these may represent three or more generations: in the last 30 years the kennel has maintained continuous breeding lines.

Gulliagh kennel was established in 1965 when Ch Ardgour of Nendrum (GB Ch Sanctuary Brave Knight ex Ch Corrie of Nendrum) was acquired from Miss Noreen Twyman. A brother of Eaglescrag Alice of Nendrum, who appears behind much of the well-known Eaglescrag stock of the 1970s, he was a tall, sound, big-bodied hound, bearing the great typical head inherited from both parents. Shortly afterwards, Ballykelly Mary, a red brindle, came from Sheelagh Seale, and the two litters from this combination formed the foundation of the kennel.

A lovely bitch, Crede of Gulliagh, was kept, but failed to breed when put to Betty Murphy's import, Ch Boroughbury Justice. As a consequence, a puppy by Justice out of Erindale Vanda, bred by the Reillys of Kiltimagh, Co Mayo, was obtained. This was Merlin, later to become Int Ch Carrokeel Coilte Merlin, an ultra-sound and well-balanced hound, again carrying a great head, well-known on both islands. He gained 17 CCs, including one at Crufts in 1979, BOB at Crufts in 1980 and at the Irish Wolfhound Club (Great Britain) Championship Show in 1979 and 1981.

In 1976 Merlin was mated to Gulliagh Falcarragh, a sister of Crede belonging to Sheelagh Seale. This produced Gulliagh Ballykelly Cait. When she was taken to Mrs Kenis-Pordham's GB Ch Eaglescrag Lysander, a litter ensued from which was retained Int Ch Gulliagh Galleon, a powerful, fairly leggy but well-boned stallion of a male with a wonderful head on a long arching neck. He was absolutely sound in movement and had great presence.

At this point a rich seam was struck by the line-breeding of Merlin daughters with Merlin's grandson, Galleon (see page 30). There came to Galleon a pair of Merlin daughters who produced some of the best-known British and Irish stock of the late 1980s and early 1990s. From the Hydebeck kennel, GB Ch Hydebeck Ballycarrie (a classically-headed, elegant bitch out of a daughter of Int Ch Erindale Triston) produced in 1985 both Int Ch Hydebeck Reginald Snuffson and Ch Hydebeck Nessa of Gulliagh. Reginald held the position of top winning Wolfhound in Britain for three consecutive years, including BOB at Crufts 1989. Meanwhile, another Merlin granddaughter with an Erindale background, Mrs Forret's Culvercroft Alanna, had come to Galleon. From this combination issued a male who was to become the winning counterpart of Reginald in Ireland: Int Ch Culvercroft Benjamin of Gulliagh. Benjamin was the Irish National Champion (top points scorer) for the three years up to 1990 and went BOB at the Crufts Centenary 1991 out of a record entry of 197. He carried the correct typical head inherited from his Eaglescrag/Sanctuary forebears and was a wonderfully balanced hound, retaining shape perfectly on the move.

The Gulliagh kennel has introduced outcross blood in recent years. Whysper of Lainston (a daughter of GB Ch Royden Quail) was acquired in 1984 and her granddaughter, Ch Gulliagh Isolde, when mated with Benjamin produced the elegant Ch Gulliagh Nadia. Yvonne von der Alten Veste, imported from Germany in 1988, has brought to the kennel some valuable traits, including her long but very well-boned legs. Various possible combinations with the existing closely-bred stock now exist, providing an interesting future for the kennel.

On average, Gulliagh kennel breeds every couple of years, and then only with a view to keeping new stock. The Finneys have always tried to retain their original Nendrum/Eaglescrag/Sanctuary lines, especially the head type, while endeavouring to improve particular points of conformation. In a breed where good males are rare, the kennel has been notably successful in producing first rate ones. They prefer a Wolfhound of the correct height, not necessarily massive, particularly in his early years, but who has good sighthound shape and excellent movement.

Int Ch Gulliagh Galleon.

Gulliagh hounds often look at their best around five to six years of age, and this is when many of their biggest show wins have been achieved. Longevity is another feature of this kennel, where only a couple of hounds have been lost under nine years of age in 30 years.

Timothy and Marion are international judges of hounds and toy breeds. Timothy has served the Irish Wolfhound Club for many years as Treasurer, and at present Marion is Secretary of the Irish Wolfhound Club of Northern Ireland.

Athcarne – Tony and Ger Redmond

In the early 1970s, Coill Tomair Maeve joined the Redmond household in a lovely cottage in the grounds of the ruined Athcarne Castle. Maeve, a well-made, free-moving bitch of marvellous temperament, bred from Ballykelly stock by Mr P Thunder, was to be the Redmonds' introduction to showing and breeding.

Maeve did not gain her title but proved her quality as a brood bitch by producing champions in both her litters, the first by Ch Ballykelly Reamon, the next by Ch Boroughbury Justice, from which the lovely Athcarne Shiofra was kept. Of beautiful type and quality, and with effortless movement, she soon gained her title. She was mated twice to GB Ch Outhwaite Am Cu, and each litter produced top show-winning progeny, all with great coursing and hunting ability. Athcarne Fintan was retained and, although used sparingly at stud, passed on his exceptional movement and love of the chase. Neesha was kept from the second litter. Although seldom shown, she won the Bitch Green Star on St Patrick's Day before being mated to Carrokeel Kalypso to continue the line of winners.

Athcarne Coolbreaugh Crana.
Photo: E C Murphy

As well as serving on the Irish Wolfhound Club Committee until recently, Tony Redmond has for several years worked tirelessly running the Wolfhound Rescue Service, to such effect that more homes than hounds are usually available. Although pressures of work and an active young family restrict Tony and Ger to very limited showing, the Athcarne hounds are much sought after around the world for their athletic type, quality, excellent heads and coats.

Other Irish kennels

The foregoing are probably the best-known Irish kennels, chosen because many kennels in other countries are likely to have stock from or pedigrees that feature at least one of their affixes. Other breeders of important hounds from the late 1960s were Mr and Mrs Bremner, who carefully bred the imposing Newtownhill hounds on the old lines, and the O'Dwyers of the Moll Machie affix. Neither

Int Ch Mary of Nutstown.

kennel is still active. Mrs Maureen Haughey with the St Doulaghs hounds made her mark in the show ring at this time and still breeds quality hounds.

The Tolkavalley affix of Miss Isobel Walton has long been synonymous with rangy, sound, athletic hounds that have always done well in the show ring and are still exhibited and occasionally bred. Billy Clarke of the Coolbreagh affix and, from Northern Ireland, Sue Rathbone Scott of Tullygirvan kennels have not bred or shown for some time, although their stock has been much sought after and very influential in many breeding programmes both here and abroad.

Many larger kennels are justifiably envious of Jim Behan of the Bearna Bui affix who, since his first litter in 1978 from the top class foundation bitch Int Ch Mary of Nutstown, is renowned for the quality of the bitches he has bred and kept from each subsequent generation to perpetuate his valuable line of champions. These include Ch Brigid of Bearna Bui, Ch Genevieve of Bearna Bui, and her daughter Int Ch Jacinta of Bearna Bui, who is by GB Ch Eaglescrag Justin and proudly owned by John and Maureen Walsh. Her brother Bearna Bui John gained his Swiss title, and another litter-mate, Gallaghan, was Top Winning Dog in France in 1994. From very limited breeding this kennel always produces quality, sought-after puppies, while Jim is frequently in demand as a handler with a special gift of getting the very best out of any hound. He has also been Chairman of the Irish Wolfhound Club for some years.

Of the Irish kennels who have not yet been breeding long enough to have established their own line fully, the Calcara hounds (based on Nutstown) of Anne O'Keeffe-Donlon are fast making their mark in the show ring both here and in

England. Calcara hounds are very distinctive and much admired for their quality, size and free movement.

ENGLAND

The following are undoubtedly the most famous and influential of the long-established English kennels, although with the exception of Eaglescrag, they are no longer active. These bloodlines can be found in the pedigrees of Irish Wolfhounds currently being shown and bred in Great Britain and have influenced a great many kennels in Ireland and the rest of the world.

Sulhamstead – Mrs Florence Nagle

Universally acknowledged as the doyenne of the breed, Florence was born in October 1894, the only daughter in the family of dairy magnate Baronet Sir William and Lady Watson. Having finished her education in France, she already owned her first Irish Wolfhound when she met and married an Irishman, James Nagle, during the First World War. James Nagle had owned Wolfhounds for some time, providing the foundation of the Sulhamstead kennels that his wife was to develop so very successfully.

Because of feeding restrictions, only one litter was bred during that war, but it included a very important future stud dog, Sulhamstead Pedlar, who sired Mr Everett's unbeaten 97cm (37½in) tall GB Ch Felixtowe Kilcullen. Pedlar was also the grandsire of Sulhamstead Dan, who was exported to the USA and proved himself invaluable as the ancestor of many top-class American hounds. At this time, Mrs Bruce Lockhart owned one of the very best brood bitches: Caragh, dam of the Nagles' first champions, GB Ch Sulhamstead Thelma and GB Ch Sulhamstead Concarra, and also of GB Ch Clodagh and GB Ch Acushla of Ouborough. Thelma was sired by Comberford Mick and Concarra by Felixtowe Kilbarry, litter-brother to Kilcullen.

GB Ch Conncara was one of the greatest sires ever in the breed and his name features many times in most Wolfhound pedigrees. He was tall at 91cm (36in), with great quality, type and soundness, and it was only when he retired from the show ring that Mrs Nagle revealed that he was blind. Bred by Mrs Lockhart, he was to have been put down, but Mrs Nagle thought him such an outstanding puppy that she took him home. Throughout his stud career he never sired a blind puppy, and he was responsible for such great champions as Galleon of Ouborough.

Between the Wars GB Ch Sulhamstead Fella (by GB Ch Fonab of Ouborough) was one of the best dogs in the kennels, winning the CC and Brewers Cup for the Best Hound at Birmingham Show at only 10 months old. His sister Sulhamstead Fara went to America and, having won her title, went on to produce some excellent hounds.

Mrs Nagle's policy was always to breed very closely to The Kennel Club Breed Standard, continually working to improve her own stock and absolutely insistent on soundness and the ability to work and hunt as nature intended. All her hounds had a great deal of exercise and, no matter how much help she had in the kennels, she always insisted on feeding puppies herself. She seldom went to other kennels for stud services, but did use GB Ch Sanctuary Rory of Kihone and GB Ch Sanctuary Brave Knight and acquired GB Ch Sulhamstead Sedlestan Rebel and Sulhamstead Sedlestan Rouletta, litter-mates by the American import Am Ch Cragwood Barney O'Shea of Riverlawn, to give new blood to her stock.

Although Sulhamstead hounds took all possible honours and broke all records in the show ring, winning was not Mrs Nagle's great concern. She believed it important to exhibit any hound she considered of sufficient quality, type and soundness. She was always very sporting in the ring and encouraging to those whose hounds she felt were unjustifiably overlooked. Amongst the countless Sulhamstead champions were Match, Minstrel, Mirth, Mogul, Medina, Motto, Remus and Romulus, to name just a few who gained their titles in England. Many more throughout the world were bred by this great kennel, which has the distinction of producing the only Irish Wolfhound ever to go BIS at Crufts: GB Ch Sulhamstead Merman (see page 38) achieved this historic win in 1960, having gone BOB in the Wolfhound classes, judged that day by Henry Fottrell, Chairman of the Irish Kennel Club and himself a distinguished Irish Wolfhound breeder. Merman was a son of GB Ch Sulhamstead Sedlestan Rebel out of GB Ch Sulhamstead Melba, who was by GB Ch Sanctuary Rory of Kihone. Some years later Mrs Nagle was to express a certain amount of regret at that great win because she felt it brought too much attention and popularity to the breed.

Apart from her great success with Wolfhounds, Florence Nagle kept Irish Terriers and was also very well-known for the Sulhamstead Irish Setters she bred for working and showing, producing 18 field trial champions, a number of whom also did well in the show ring. She was instrumental in the revival of the Irish Red and White Setter, allowing her Irish Setters (whom she did not mind carrying a little white) be used at stud to give a much-needed boost to the gene pool that got the older breed going again. She also bred some extremely good flat-race horses, Sandsprite finishing second in the 1937 Derby, and she became notorious when, in 1966, she took the English Jockey Club to court and won the right for women to be licensed to train horses. She was again in the limelight in 1978 when she had The Kennel Club up before an Industrial Tribunal, claiming sex-discrimination against women and gaining for them the right to become full members of that august body. She was certainly not a feminist, but a firm believer in equality who had no fear of fighting for what she believed was just.

For many years she was Chairman of the Irish Wolfhound Club before resigning to become a Founder Member and Chair of the Irish Wolfhound Society; she also chaired the Ladies Kennel Association for 19 years. She was in great demand as a judge all over the world, and officiated at the first ever Irish Breeds Society Show, held in Ireland.

Although considered by many a formidable and autocratic lady, to those who knew her well she showed great kindness and a wicked sense of humour, often against herself. She invariably gave very generously of her time, knowledge and the use of her stud dogs to serious newcomers to the breed, but was so often taken

Mrs Nagle with GB Ch Sulhamstead Motto and friends.

Mrs Elsie James with Montebello Prince of Boroughbury and Boroughbury Alewa.
Courtesy of A Killykeen-Doyle.

advantage of and misquoted that she tended, in public, to present a very reserved and unapproachable front. Even before the end of the 1970s she was worried that the breed was becoming too popular, falling into the hands of people with insufficient understanding and dedication to raise and breed hounds of the correct size and conformation. She felt that the quality and soundness of hounds was being lost and the standard of judging deteriorating.

The shock of the sudden death of her son, David, in the summer of 1987, took its toll on Mrs Nagle, and she herself died in December 1988. For those who knew her, learnt from her wealth of knowledge and experience and extensively tapped into her stock, her influence will be everlasting. It would be her fervent hope that her protégés and devotees would continue to uphold her ideals of breeding sound, fit, workman-like, quality Irish Wolfhounds.

Boroughbury – Mrs Elsie James

Elsie James was Irish by birth, a daughter of the Latchfords of County Kerry, established landowners and millers. She attended the same veterinary college as Miss Twyman, with whom she was very friendly, but left to get married and settle in England just before her final examination.

Mrs James acquired her first Wolfhound in the late 1930s from the Ouborough kennels, and she also had stock from Mrs Fitzgibbons (Artel) and from Miss Nichols of the Bradfield kennels. In 1944 Elsie James mated her Clonboy of Ouborough with the strangely-named bitch Kevin of Ouborough, producing her first English and Irish Champion, Mulligan of Boroughbury. Mulligan's litter brother, GB Ch McCarthy of Ouborough, went to Mr Rank. Clonboy was to prove a great and influential stud dog, whilst Artel Felclarion was a very important brood bitch. Mated together they produced the very well-known Int Ch Artel Ballykelly Sandy. Int Ch Mulligan of Boroughbury sired GB Ch Ouborough Tara of Boroughbury, who was the cornerstone of the post-war kennels.

After the war Mrs James was inactive for some years, neither breeding nor showing hounds. Then she began to work closely with Sheelagh Seale, some of whose Ballykelly stock was only two generations removed from her own original lines. One of the first bitches she bred was Boroughbury Brona, who took her English title before going to Sam Ewing in America and becoming an important factor in his Eagle kennels. She also used Sulhamstead, Eaglescrag and Nendrum dogs to continue her breeding

Elsie James was a very kind and gentle lady, a great stockwoman and judge with a deep love and knowledge of Wolfhounds. Having been out of the breed for several years, she wrote in her notes that it came as something of a shock to her, when judging the club open show in 1980, to find how the quality, type and soundness of many of the hounds bred by newcomers had degenerated. In their heyday the Boroughbury hounds were distinguished by their quality, size, soundness and good temperament, which was of paramount importance to Mrs James, one of the great breeders. She died, aged 77, in October 1987.

Sanctuary – Miss Harrison and Miss Atfield

With her sister, Beatrice, Margaret Harrison was known internationally as a great and talented musician, much in demand for concerts, cello and violin recitals and master classes. Wolfhounds, mainly from the neighbouring Ouborough kennels, had been in her family for many years. May Atfield went to live and work with Miss Harrison and, at the outset of the Second World War, they cared for the dogs belonging to the airmen while they were flying or when they failed to return – hence the name *Sanctuary*. Apart from Wolfhounds, they bred Pomeranians and Pekinese.

After the war Miss F J McGregor sent Rory of Kihone from America as a gift to the Irish Wolfhound Club. Once out of quarantine he went to live at the Sanctuary kennels, proving a very important sire of champions and foundation stock for other kennels and easily gaining his English title. Not a big dog, but of great type and quality, being very sound and an excellent mover, he was responsible for saving the breed and improving temperament, which had become a problem. Later he was joined by another American dog, Mrs Van Brunt's Am Ch Cragwood Barney O'Shea.

By breeding carefully for true type and to the Breed Standard the kennel

Mrs Nagle with BIS Crufts 1969: GB Ch Sulhamstead Merman.
Courtesy of A Killykeen-Doyle.

achieved great success and the distinctive Sanctuary hounds became well-known for their particularly beautiful heads and excellent temperaments. In 1964 Sanctuary Brave Knight was the first of many home-bred champions, including GB Ch Sanctuary Monica (his daughter), GB Ch Sanctuary Revog who won the coveted Graham Shield and a Hound Group, and GB Ch Sanctuary Mona who was BOB at Crufts. Sanctuary Wolfhounds were much sought after by breeders and many hounds went abroad, gained their titles and contributed much as breeding stock.

Miss Atfield died in 1979, but Miss Harrison continued with the kennels until poor health overtook her. She went to be cared for by friends in Scotland with Rua, one of the last of the typically beautiful Sanctuary hounds. A truly gentle, gracious and regal lady, Miss Margaret Harrison died on Christmas Eve 1995, well into her ninth decade, and was interred in the family grave next to the great composer, Delius.

Eaglescrag – Leslie and Ruth Jenkins

Ruth was born into a family of animal-lovers and her introduction to Wolfhounds came at a very early age with Droonagh, one of the family pets, so it was almost inevitable that she would have Wolfhounds of her own as soon as circumstances were right. This was not to be until 1950, when she and her husband, Leslie, acquired Develin Molly.

Molly was shown with some success, but was not considered of sufficient merit to be the foundation bitch of the Eaglescrag kennels. This fell to Kilfenora of Ouborough, one of the last of the great Ouborough hounds, a bitch of particularly good type, quality, soundness and temperament. The progeny of her mating with the American import GB Ch Sanctuary Rory of Kihone included Song of Eaglescrag, Sanctuary Sonnet of Eaglescrag and the famous Int Ch Carol of Eaglescrag. To each she passed on her own qualities. In time these bitches were mated to Sulhamstead dogs, each producing top-class progeny, including GB Ch Sanctuary Brave Knight, GB Ch Moira of Eaglescrag, Saragh of Eaglescrag (dam of GB Ch Clindhu and GB Ch Sulhamstead Morna of Eaglescrag) as well as GB Ch Corrie of Nendrum and GB Ch Eaglescrag Clonroe of Nendrum (BOB Crufts 1965).

Clindhu was the Jenkins' first champion, gaining his title in 1966 at the same show as Moira – a great 'double'. Moira's son by Clonroe, GB Ch Red Wully, was a wonderful ambassador for the breed, doing a lot of advertising work and travelling frequently on the London Underground. Among his wins was Reserve in the Hound Group at Crufts and Reserve BIS in Scotland in 1970. From a kennel of great and influential males, GB Ch Caio of Eaglescrag (Clindhu ex Alice) was considered one of the best; amongst his many wins, in 1974 he took BOB from the Veteran class, going on to win the Hound Group.

Never short of top-class bitches, Mrs Jenkins considers GB Ch Eaglescrag Celeste (the seventh generation of this kennel's breeding) one of the best hounds she has bred; she is dam of the beautiful GB Ch Eaglescrag Iceflo. Her sister Cariad has produced GB Ch Eaglescrag Harvester as well as GB Ch Eaglescrag Jake and GB Ch Eaglescrag Justin. Iceflo was mated to GB Ch Telgar Hadlee to produce the magnificent GB Ch Eaglescrag Kapitan, who won the Hound Group

GB Ch Conchessa of Eaglescrag with judge Margaret Harrison
at the Hound Show 1969.

at the South Wales Show in 1993 and 1994, when he also went BIS. To date, no less than 20 English Champions have been bred and shown by this great kennel.

The Jenkins have always considered bone, size, sound conformation and good temperament essential when breeding – qualities much evident in all Eaglescrag hounds. Many have gone overseas to found new kennels, the best-known of these being: the Fitzarran kennels of Mr and Mrs Deemer, top breeders in the United States; the Oelmühle kennels of Messrs Pappenfuss and Rosner in Germany; the Wolf Tone kennels of Elisabeth and Leif Janzon in Sweden; and the Tirowen kennels of Mr and Mrs McEvoy in Australia.

Ruth Jenkins has worked tirelessly for the Irish Wolfhound Club for many years: on Committee since 1966, Chairman for seven years and now a Vice-President. In 1967 she and three colleagues set up the Irish Wolfhound Rescue Trust, which to date has re-homed or cared for about 1000 hounds. Much in demand as a judge, Mrs Jenkins has twice officiated at the American Specialty – a rare honour. Now almost retired from showing and judging, Ruth Jenkins is of that very rare breed: a genuinely kind, caring person, unfailingly helpful to newcomers and a great sport in the show ring, always first to congratulate anyone placed higher than herself.

Brabyns – Ms Susanne Hudson

Although her parents, Captain and Mrs Hudson, kept a large kennel of Wolfhounds in the 1920s and 1930s and were known for producing a very active, hunting type, Susanne did not have a Wolfhound of her own until her wandering, Romany-like lifestyle brought her in the 1960s to Ireland and her friend, Sheelagh Seale. From her she bought a bitch puppy, Ballykelly O'Flynn, who grew up to take both her Irish and English titles.

Returning to England in 1966, Susanne settled in Norfolk, inherited her father's Brabyns affix and once again built up a prominent kennel of workman-like hounds. O'Flynn was mated to Ch Clindhu of Eaglescrag, producing winning progeny, and through the Boroughbury lines came Feccna of Brabyns who sired six English champions, including the very well-known Int Ch Petasmeade Chieftain of Brabyns, himself the father of outstanding stock both here and abroad, prominent in many pedigrees, and grandsire of Susanne's last champion, Fiona of Brabyns (born in 1980). Brabyns Breagha (Brabyns Slainte ex Blaithnaith of Brabyns) proved to be a wonderful brood bitch, producing eight continental and one Canadian champion.

Susanne Hudson was a very independent and colourful character, well-known for her artistic and literary talents. In her youth she gained a Diploma from the Royal Academy, London, and she has written and published beautifully illustrated books on the breed. Strong-minded and uncompromising as a judge, she severely penalised heavily-built, unathletic hounds and had no fear of dismissing big winners if they seemed incapable of hunting. Having retired from breeding, she returned to live in Ireland and, after her death in 1996, her ashes were interred close to those of her mentor, Miss Seale.

Brabyns Gerland of Eaglescrag with passenger.
Courtesy of A Killykeen-Doyle.

Jason of Sunningdale.
Photo: F E Garwood, *Dog World*

Erindale – Mrs Marjorie Saunders

Always dog lovers, Marjorie and Roy Saunders came into the breed in 1970 more by accident than design, when they were offered a Wolfhound bitch, as her owner was becoming too frail to cope. Having retired from a very successful business life they moved to Sunningdale Farm to open a small boarding kennel.

The 'rescue' bitch, bred in Ireland by Dr May, was Brid of Ballytobin, a truly beautiful hound who had been crippled by a broken leg. Her pedigree (Ch Connel of Nendrum ex Maeve of Dunamaise) made her a worthy and important brood bitch and, mated to Sanctuary Knight of Kerry, she produced two US champions as well as Jason of Sunningdale in her first litter. A great stud dog and sire of five English champions, Jason was unshown because he had been surgically docked. Brid's second litter to GB Ch Sanctuary Revog gave Marjorie GB Ch Erindale Bernice, the first of a great many Erindale bitch champions here and abroad.

Probably the most notable hound of the mid 1970s was a grandson of Jason, Int Ch Erindale Triston. Closely line-bred based on Sanctuary, he was tall and well-angulated with a quality head and very impressive. As the top winning dog in both England and Ireland he was much in demand at stud. His progeny have been phenomenally successful, GB Ch Erindale Clarion of Finloren, GB Ch Lady Sacha and GB Ch Erindale Callan of Finloren being among those home-bred, and he invariably uplifted any bitch sent to him. He sired eight champions from eight different bitches and in 1983 was not only Top Wolfhound Stud Dog, but Top Stud in the Hound Group and second in the British Stud Dog of the Year All Breeds. A great number of overseas champions carry the Erindale affix, and a dog from one of Triston's last litters, GB Ch Kellybourne Pilot at Ballalyn, was a multi-Group Winner and, in 1984, Top Irish Wolfhound and Pro Dog of the Year.

Marjorie and Roy eventually gave up breeding and showing for retirement by the sea, but they undoubtedly ran one of the most successful and influential Wolfhound kennels during their time in the breed. Many currently-active kennels were fortunate in having use of Erindale stud dogs and bitches for foundation stock. Sadly, Roy died recently, and is greatly missed by all who knew him

Drakesleat – Ms Zena Thorn-Andrews

Of the top personalities currently active in breeding and showing, Zena Thorn-Andrews with the long-established Drakesleat hounds is without doubt the most successful. Her first Irish Wolfhound, Edgecroft Simon (born 1967), was by Sanctuary Domenick out of a bitch of Ballykelly parentage. He was the first of a great number of champions from this kennel. In 1976, Ch Edgecroft Simon's

GB Ch Sovryn of Drakesleat. Photo: Sally Anne Thompson

daughter, Drakesleat D-Day, was mated to GB Ch Sulhamstead Motto, and this union produced two English champions, Roisin and Runen, and South African Ch Drakesleat Ragdas. Drakesleat D-Day was an extremely important bitch because, when mated to Ard Choille of Rannochlea (a son of GB Ch Red Wully of Eaglescrag), her daughter, Musyk, was retained and, when mated with GB Ch Drakesleat Runen, produced a dog many top judges and breeders describe as one of the best Irish Wolfhounds ever: GB Ch Drakesleat Kyak.

GB Ch Drakesleat Kyak, who died in 1984, is still the breed record holder, with over 40 CCs and more Group and BIS wins than any other Wolfhound. His son, GB Ch Sovryn of Drakesleat (see page 43), remains the top sire of all time, with a great many winning grandchildren currently in the ring. The most famous of these is GB Ch Drakesleat Odyt (see page 142) who took Reserve BIS at Crufts in 1993 – an outstanding placing, surpassed only by Mrs Nagle's BIS at Crufts 1960 with Ch Sulhamstead Merman.

From its founding, the Drakesleat kennel has had a remarkable show career. To date there are 20 English champions and at least as many overseas champions. Since GB Ch Drakesleat Roisin and GB Ch Drakesleat Runen left the ring there has been at least one Drakesleat hound in the top five winning hounds in Great Britain every year. Zena Thorn-Andrews is justifiably credited with producing some of the most sound and typical Wolfhounds around today and has the distinction of making the Drakesleat kennel the second top-winning kennel of all time, her friend and mentor Mrs Nagle retaining top place with the famous Sulhamstead hounds.

Other English kennels

Many English kennels have been registered in the past 20 years, some breeding and showing with more success than others. The Buckhurst, Royden and Witchesbroom kennels are no longer active but had an enormous influence during the 1970s. Each produced hounds of distinctive type, quality and virtues important to the breed and was much appreciated and used.

Mr and Mrs Baird founded the Outhwaite kennel in the late 1960s and, from very limited breeding, produced a high proportion of champions and influential stud dogs. Mrs Innes bred and showed good Petasmeade hounds; Joy Duggan first registered her Pendomers affix in the mid-1960s and, although never subjecting her own to the show ring, produced many quality hounds who went on to gain their titles with other enthusiasts in England and abroad, and to found successful new kennels, including Owenmore.

Rosemary Follet (Edeyrn) produced top-class hounds based on Sulhamstead stock during the 1970s and 1980s. Sulhamstead stock is also behind Maggie Wilkins' very sound, typical, harsh-coated Clonara (Clonmagara) hounds. An infusion of blood from these kennels invariably proves a valuable addition to a pedigree. At the same time, Gordon Crane was breeding and showing the important, influential, workman-like Seplecur hounds, based on similar bloodlines.

Int Ch Kellybourne Pilot at Ballalyn. Photo: David Dalton

GB Ch Erindale Callan of Finloren, owned by Shirley Sharpe. Photo: Diane Pearce

Elizabeth Till (Thornton) bred her first litter under the Mochras affix in the early 1970s from her foundation bitch Buckhurst Theresa, and Mary McBride registered her Marumac affix, which has for many years been synonymous with show ring success, with many champions here and abroad, including the particularly lovely top winning bitch GB Ch Marumac Barbarella. In many of the Marumac hounds the influence of Sanctuary and Eaglescrag is very evident.

Louise Nowell, starting with Erindale hounds, established the distinctive and distinguished Hydebeck line. One of her best dogs was Int Ch Hydebeck Reginald Snuffson, a great show dog and sire of many top-class winners. Also from Erindale stock, the Bokra kennels of Sandra Surrell and Cathy Coleman have for many years now been producing very shapely and attractive hounds, using stud dogs from Witchesbroom, Eaglescrag and Drakesleat.

Lyn and Dennis McMillan, although coming into the breed a little later, consistently take top honours in the show ring with their particularly well-presented Ballalyn Wolfhounds, GB Ch Ballalyns Himself (another of Drakesleat Sovryn's grandsons) taking BOB at Crufts 1995.

These are just a very few of the established English kennels consistent in selective line-breeding and with distinctive and proven stock. Between them they have bred and continue to breed a high proportion of top-quality hounds. Many of their puppies are exported and shown with great success in other countries before taking up breeding duties, either blending in with established and proven stock as valuable outcrosses or founding new lines.

Pendomers Will o' the Wisp. Photo: Frank Garwood

CHAPTER THREE

A good Irish Wolfhound head: Killykeen Jermyma.
Photo: Robert Smith

IRISH WOLFHOUND BREED STANDARD

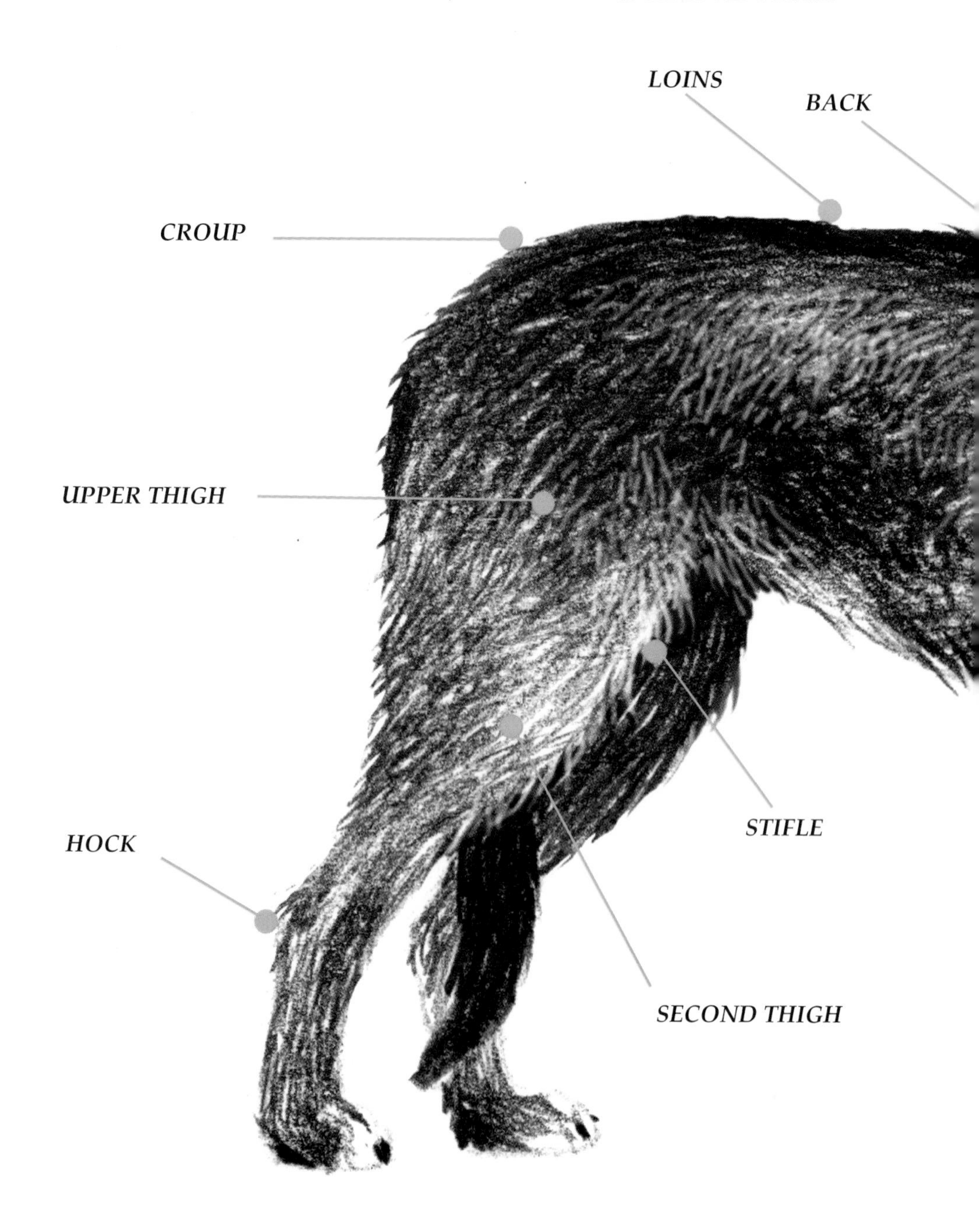

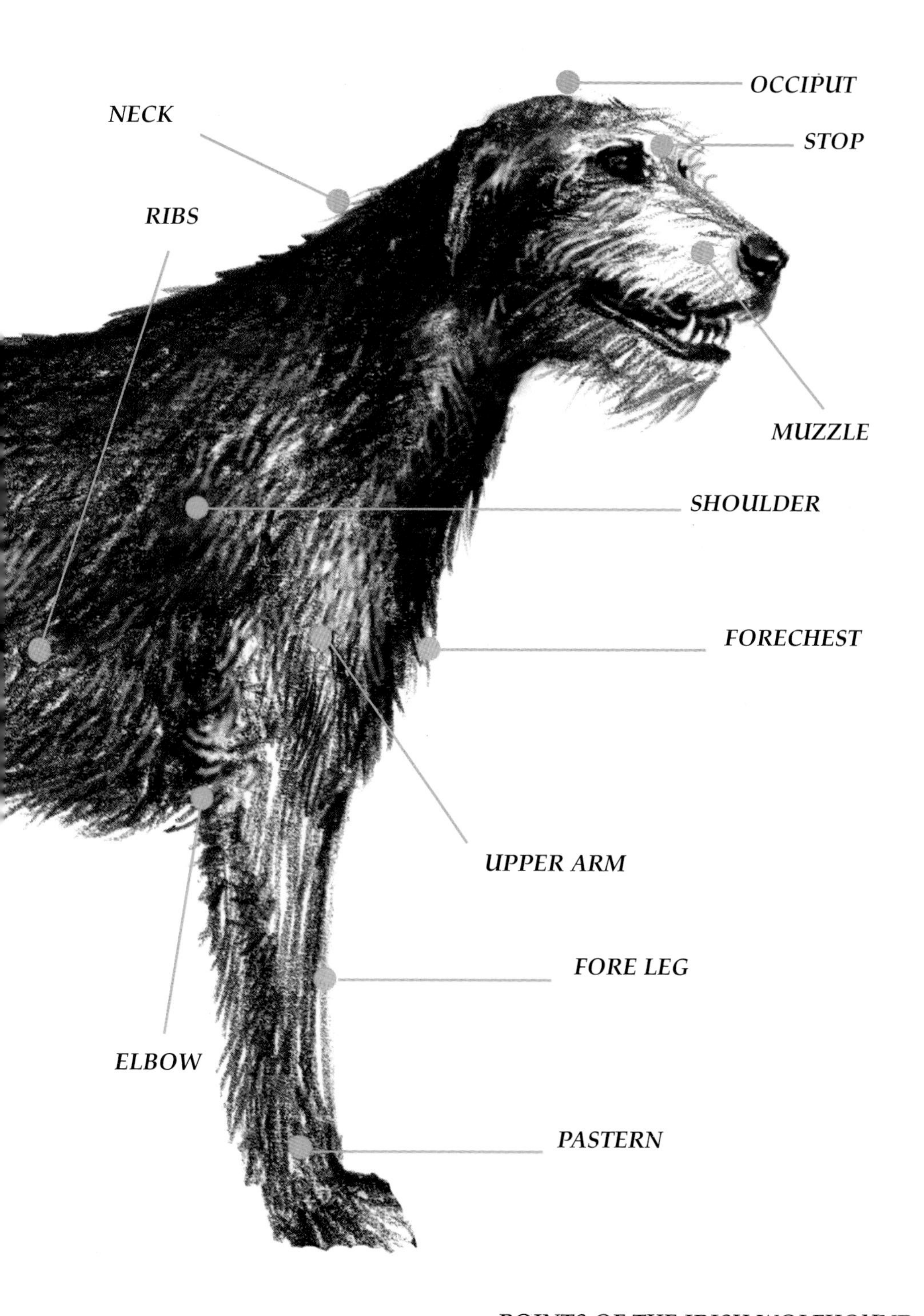

POINTS OF THE IRISH WOLFHOUND

Irish Wolfhound Standard of Excellence

(Courtesy of the Irish Wolfhound Club of Ireland)

1 **General Appearance:** The Irish Wolfhound should not be quite so heavy or massive as the Great Dane, but more so than the Deerhound, which in general type he should otherwise resemble. Of great size and commanding appearance, very muscular, strongly though gracefully built, movements easy and active; head and neck carried high; the tail carried with an upward sweep with a slight curve towards the extremity.

The minimum height and weight of dogs should be 31in (79cm) and 120lb (54.5kg); of bitches, 28in (71cm) and 90lb (40.9kg). Anything below this should be debarred from competition. Great size, including height at shoulder and proportionate length of body, is the desideratum to be aimed at, and it is desired to firmly establish a race that shall average from 32–34in (81–86cm) in dogs, showing the requisite power, activity, courage and symmetry.

2 **Head:** Long, the frontal bones of the forehead very slightly raised and very little indentation between the eyes. Skull, not too broad. Muzzle, long and moderately pointed, ears small and greyhound-like in carriage. Bite, scissors ideal, level acceptable.

3 **Neck:** Rather long, very strong and muscular, well arched, without dewlap or loose skin about the throat.

4 **Chest:** Very deep. Breast wide.

5 **Back:** Rather long than short. Loins arched.

6 **Tail:** Long and slightly curved, of moderate thickness, and well covered with hair.

7 **Belly:** Well drawn up.

8 **Forequarters:** Shoulders muscular, giving breadth of chest, set sloping. Elbows well under, neither turned inwards nor outwards. Leg – Forearm muscular, and the whole leg strong and quite straight.

9 **Hindquarters:** Muscular thighs and second thigh long and strong as in the Greyhound, and hocks well let down and turning neither in nor out.

10 **Feet:** Moderately large and round, neither turned inwards nor outwards. Toes, well arched and closed. Nails very strong and curved.

11 **Hair:** Tough and hard on body, legs and head; especially wiry and long over eyes and under jaw.

12 **Colour and Markings:** The recognised colours are grey, brindle, red, black, pure white, fawn, or any colour that appears in the Deerhound.

13 **Faults:** Too light or too heavy a head, too highly arched frontal bone; large ears and hanging flat to the face; short neck; full dewlap; too narrow or too broad chest; sunken or hollow or quite straight back; bent forelegs; overbent fetlocks; twisted feet; spreading toes; too curly a tail; weak hindquarters and general

Wolfhounds come in various colours: (from left) grey brindle, cream, red, light grey.

want of muscle; too short in body; pink or liver-coloured eyelids; lip and nose any colour other than black; very light eyes.

The Irish Wolfhound Club of Ireland appends the **List of Points in Order of Merit** to the Standard, considering it to be of great use and importance:

List of Points in Order of Merit

1 Typical: The Irish Wolfhound should not be quite so heavy or massive as the Great Dane, but more so than the Deerhound, which in general type he should otherwise resemble.

2 Great size and commanding appearance.

3 Movements easy and active.

4 Head, long and level, carried high.

5 Forelegs, heavily boned, quite straight; elbows well set under.

6 Thighs long and muscular; second thighs, well muscled, stifles nicely bent.

7 Coat, rough and hard, especially wiry and long over the eyes and under jaw.

8 Body, long, well ribbed up, with ribs well sprung, and great breadth across hips.

9 Loins arched, belly well drawn up.

10 Ears, small, with Greyhound-like carriage.

11 Feet, moderately large and round; toes close, well arched.

12 Neck, long, well arched and very strong.

13 Chest, very deep, moderately broad.

14 Shoulders, muscular, set sloping.

15 Tail, long and slightly curved.

16 Eyes, dark.

Note: The above in no way alters the Standard of Excellence, which must in all cases be rigidly adhered to; they simply give the various points in order of merit. If in any case they appear at variance with the Standard of Excellence, it is the latter which is correct.

The foregoing is very close to the original Official Standard drawn up by Captain Graham, Major Garnier and Mr J F Baily in 1885 and is the one adhered to by the Irish Wolfhound Club of Ireland. The Fédèration Cynologique Internationale (FCI) also insists that its member countries judge to this as it is their policy to abide by the Breed Standard of the country of origin. The American Kennel Club adopted some minor changes in 1950, but The Kennel Club made more drastic revisions in 1985.

Thoughts on the Irish Wolfhound Standard of Excellence

A breed standard is a blueprint – an attempt to describe the proportions and concept of the ideal specimen. It will convey a slightly different picture to all who read it, but every effort should be made fully to understand each point, and the reason why it should be so. Those who disregard or make light of the Standard are doing the breed a great disservice, and acceptance of any divergence by breeders and judges from its ideals will result in breed type being lost. Common faults

A beautiful bitch of absolutely correct type: GB Ch Witchesbroom Wildrose. Photo: Diana Pearce

being perpetuated in defiance of the Standard are short legs (with consequent loss of height), poor forehand construction, a tendency to cow hocks and a general want of musculature.

If, whilst studying the Standard of Excellence, you can picture a Wolfhound at its original work – crossing difficult, often mountainous and rocky, terrain at speed, hunting and killing wolves and other fast-moving large game – it will help to create an image of true type and possibly clarify the reason for some of the requisite points. Put out of your mind any vision of beautifully groomed, posed, show-ring hounds; the essence of the Irish Wolfhound is the remarkable combination of power, strength, speed, keen sight and innate hunting ability, all of

Great size and commanding appearance exemplified by Int Ch Erindale Triston.
Photo: F E Garwood, *Dog World*

which is suggested by its conformation and movement. The American Standard aptly describes it as *the largest and tallest of the galloping hounds, in general type a rough-coated, Greyhound-like breed.*

1 **General Appearance:** Although the first sentence of the Standard is somewhat ambiguous one must remember that the authors were referring to the Great Danes and Deerhounds of the day. The Great Dane Standard of 1883 required dogs to be a minimum height of 76cm (30in), weight 54.5kg (120lb), bitches 71cm (28in), weight 45.4kg (100lb). The Scottish Deerhound Standard of 1892 calls for dogs to be of height 71–76cm (28–30in) and weight 38.6–47.7kg (85–105lb), bitches of minimum height 66cm (26in) and weight 29.5–36.3kg (65–80lb).

   Although the desired heights for both bitches and dogs was firmly established in the early 1900s and males frequently measured over 86cm (34in),

Movement easy and active. GB Ch Eaglescrag Iceflo in the ring. Photo: Anthony Hillier-Fry

today size has undoubtedly been lost. Males of 78.7cm (31in) and less have become the norm, with bitches correspondingly smaller. *Great size and commanding appearance* in males in particular is increasingly rare, although every country has some magnificent hounds of correct height and size, even if these may not be the ones currently winning in the show ring.

Size when applied to Wolfhounds does not just mean height, but encompasses length and breadth (achieved by good bone and muscle) proportionate to height – a perfect balance of these giving the requisite power and symmetry.

Wolfhound hunting in Norway over rough, mountainous terrain.
Photo: Sjur Giljane

Int Ch Ballalyn's Dancer, showing typical, soft expression.

Commanding appearance indicates temperament. Over-friendly, fawning hounds lack *commanding appearance* just as much as those who are shy or nervous. The hound exuding quiet, confident pride and dignity will, without effort, command the attention and admiration of all around. This is what is meant by *presence*, lack of which diminishes otherwise good hounds.

Movement easy and active: This is clearly demonstrated by long, relaxed strides, effortlessly executed with grace and economy while covering a great deal of ground. A hound should appear light on its feet and indefatigable, and at all paces it should be apparent that the drive and impulsion comes from the hindquarters. At the trot, the front feet should not be lifted far off the ground, *daisy-cutting* rather than high-stepping hackney action being correct. The hocks should flex and the pads of the hind feet be visible as the hound moves away. The topline must remain level and the head be carried proudly. The trot is the pace by which movement is judged.

On the move, each leg should retain a straight column of bones from elbow to foot, which should turn neither in *(pinning)* nor out *(paddling)*, and from point of hip down through the hock to the hind foot. In a *cow-hocked* hound (see Fig 1) these joints converge, and invariably one or both hind feet turn out. Unfortunately, this weak and incorrect hind movement is now accepted by so many judges that it is becoming the norm and any hound moving well behind is an increasingly rare sight and usually penalised for moving *wide*. A much less common weakness is one or both hocks bending out when weight is applied. Although these weaknesses are not immediately detrimental to a hound's ability to move at any pace, the cumulative effect on joints causes them to break down much earlier in life than would otherwise be the case – disaster in a hunting breed characterised by its speed, agility and endurance.

At a slow or collected trot the front and hind legs move almost parallel. It is only when speeding up to an extended or fast trot that the legs converge towards the centre line under the body and the hound will nearly single track.

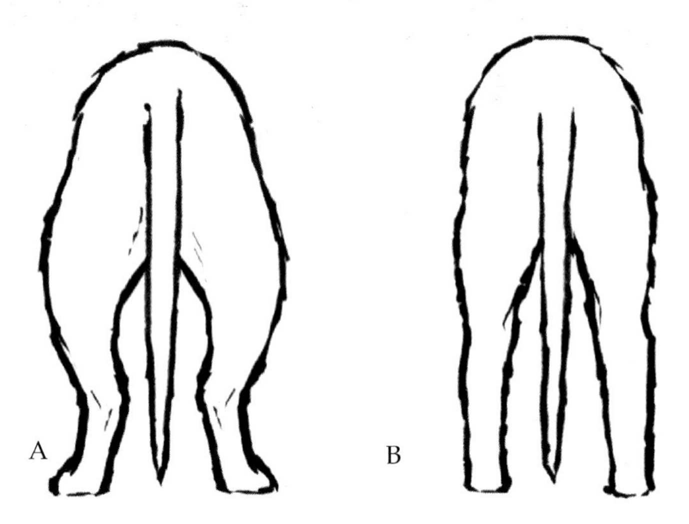

Fig 1: Structure of hindquarters and legs:
A: Cow hocks. B: Correct hocks.

2 Head: This is described in detail as it is a major point in establishing breed and type and there is little room for interpretation, although further in-depth research shows that the muzzle should be longer than the skull from stop to occiput rather than of equal length, which gives a rather 'blocky' look to the head.

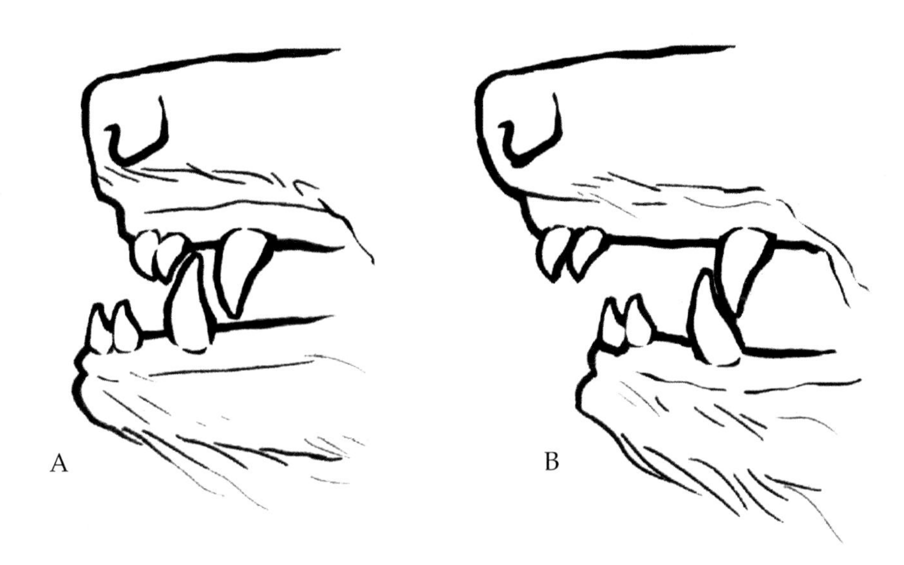

Fig 2: Incorrect jaw structure:
A: Undershot – lower incisors project beyond upper ones.
B: Overshot – upper incisors project beyond lower ones.

Eyes are not described in detail, other than very light being a fault, but to have the characteristic soft, far-off look they must be of a slight oval shape and dark. Although a light coloured eye is in no way detrimental to sight, it is far less likely to reflect the soft look, and round, staring eyes, however dark, greatly detract from any head and expression.

The *mouth* (see Fig 2) seems to cause much controversy, some judges heavily penalising a hound with a dropped or crooked incisor while overlooking poor conformation or appalling movement. The Standard specifies scissors bite with level acceptable. No mention is made of crooked incisors, a triviality which does not in any way affect the mouth's function. Obviously incorrect jaw construction (overshot, undershot, crooked and so on) with the resulting misalignment of teeth is a very serious fault, which could adversely affect a hound's ability to hold onto and kill its prey, and any predisposition to very small or missing teeth should certainly be bred away from. Unlike a terrier, which relies on a single, fatal bite to kill vicious prey, the hound usually kills by breaking the neck or back of its victim with a quick flick or shake; therefore, absolutely perfect dentition is not of prime importance in fulfilling its function.

3 Neck: This is extremely important in the chase and kill, and the angle at which it fits into the body is critical in facilitating sighthound functions such as raising the head to spot quarry, reaching out to pull down a wolf, or up for the neck of large deer or elk. In times past, the Wolfhound was expected to have the strength and reach to pull a man from a fast-moving horse, so the neck must be extremely powerful, the muscles creating a nice arch or crest. It should not be too long or it will lose strength and be in danger of dislocation in combat; nor does it need be as long as that of a Greyhound who must reach to the ground for rabbits and hares and despatches only small game. At speed the neck is used for balance and, if set too high, prevents lowering of the head and so inhibits efficient galloping and effective use of scent. Although of the sighthound family, the Wolfhound uses scent to a surprising degree when hunting. A dewlap or loose skin about the throat not only spoils the line of a neck, but offers an easy hold for the hound's foe.

4 **Chest:** This needs be deep and the breast of sufficient width to allow ample heart and lung room.

5 **Back:** *Rather long than short* implies length of ribbing that houses and protects heart, lungs and other vital organs. Great lung capacity is vital for the stamina needed by a galloping, hunting hound, so it goes without saying that the ribcage should not only be of good length, but well-sprung. However, this does not mean barrel-shaped, which would impede free movement.

Loin and croup (see Fig 3) are the key part of a hound's spine when in motion. From here comes the flexibility which allows the hind legs to reach well under the body for maximum propulsion, particularly when galloping. The croup

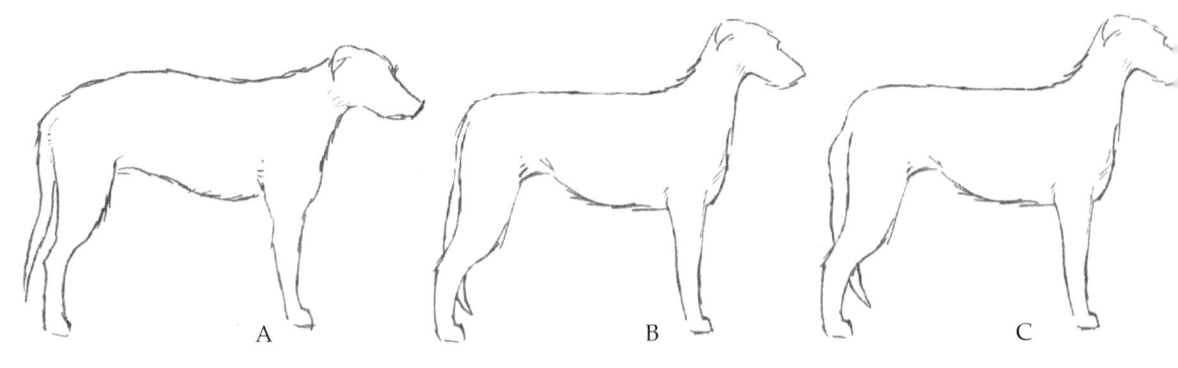

Fig 3: Loin and croup:
A: Roach back. B: Straight topline, flat croup, high tail-set. C: Steep croup, giving low tail-set.

should smoothly continue the gentle slope set by the arch of the loin and be of good width to allow the hind legs to pass outside the front legs at speed. A *roach back* (when the arch is too far forward) or too little or too much arch will be directly reflected on the hind action, as will too long or too short a loin, the one lacking strength and power, the other flexibility. A flat croup makes for a high tail-set and is often accompanied by straight or rather narrow thighs and stifles, which will shorten the stride, whilst a very steep croup is invariably compensated for by cow-hocks or turning-out of the hind feet – weaknesses that will not impair speed over short distances, but will forfeit stamina.

GB Ch Clonara Cassnu shows correct length of body and shapely topline.

6 **Tail:** If you watch a Wolfhound coursing or simply having a mad moment of irrational racing around, it will become clear why the tail needs be long and strong. It is used to great effect both as a rudder to steer and a brake when suddenly stopping, particularly if going downhill. A hound with a proportionately short or thin tail is much slower on the turn than one with a good length and weight to steer it, and any hound unfortunate enough to have lost part of its tail becomes appreciably slower and less agile on corners.

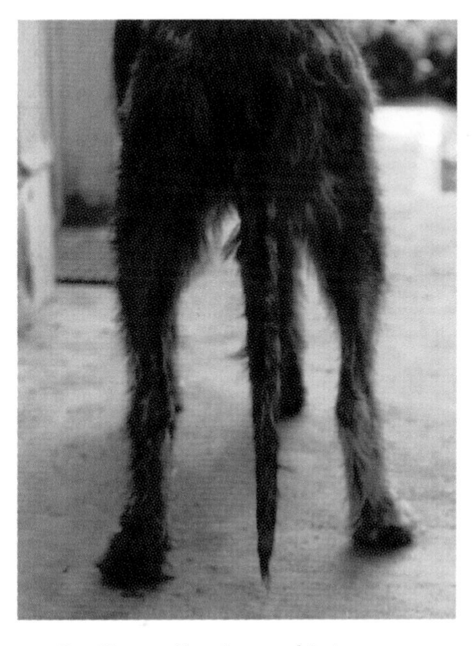

Good long tail and strong hindquarters.

7 **Belly:** This should be well drawn up to give space and freedom for the hindquarters to come forward at speed and not overload the spine or lessen flexibility.

8 **Forequarters:** These are described clearly, and Captain Graham also said, 'It is essential that the shoulders should be nicely laid back, not upright.' This is to allow freer and therefore faster action. As well as sloping back, the shoulder blades

should slope inwards, coming fairly close together at the withers, about three fingers apart being the accepted distance when the hound is standing with head raised. An upright or straight shoulder is caused by the angle between shoulder blade and upper arm being too open (see fig 4).

Although no mention is made of the *upper arm* which now figures so prominently in the breed owner's vocabulary, experts have said that the absolute ideal for freedom and ease of movement and to minimise concussion of the forequarters is for the upper arm to be of similar length to the shoulder blade

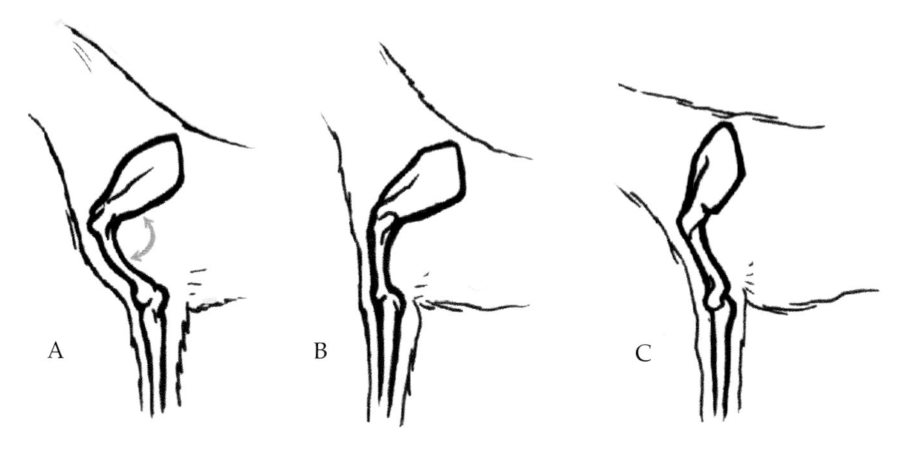

Fig 4: Structure of shoulder:
A: Correct shoulder placement. B: Short, upright upper arm. C: Straight shoulder, angle too open.

and meet it at a 90° angle, thus placing the elbow in a direct line beneath the withers. On the move this will allow great reach of stride and, when standing, the hound will be correctly balanced, with its forelegs well under, taking weight with the minimum of strain. (This degree of angulation of the forehand is extremely rare, and an angle of about 100° between the upper arm and shoulder blade is considered acceptable.)

A frequently-occurring fault is that, even though the shoulder blade may lie at the correct angle, the upper arm is rather short and upright, taking the front legs forward of the wither and giving an impression of them being 'tacked-on' to the chest. When the front legs are thus placed no forechest is visible and there is usually a dip behind the wither, making the back appear to sag. A short, straight upper arm greatly restricts movement, giving either a short stride or a 'goose-stepping' action, so the hound will tire more quickly.

The *forechest* is where the breastbone or sternum protrudes between the front legs, and should be well padded by good muscling on either side.

To cover ground with ease and minimum expenditure of energy, any galloping hound must have proportionately long *legs*. These not only constitute the greyhound look but give plenty of daylight underneath, as preferred by the old breeders. The legs should be heavily boned and well-muscled; quite straight when viewed from the front but, in side-view, sloping very slightly forward at the pasterns.

9 **Hindquarters:** These are clearly described and need to be very muscular and strong as they are responsible for propulsion. The thighs constitute the greatest single muscle mass in the whole hound and should be not only thick, but wide, to provide the requisite powerful thrusting drive for easy movement. Width should be carried on down through nicely-bent stifles, into long, muscular second thighs, to low, strong hocks that point directly backwards, inclining neither in nor out.

This Wolfhound's muzzle is too short, giving him a 'blocky' head, and his eye is rather light.

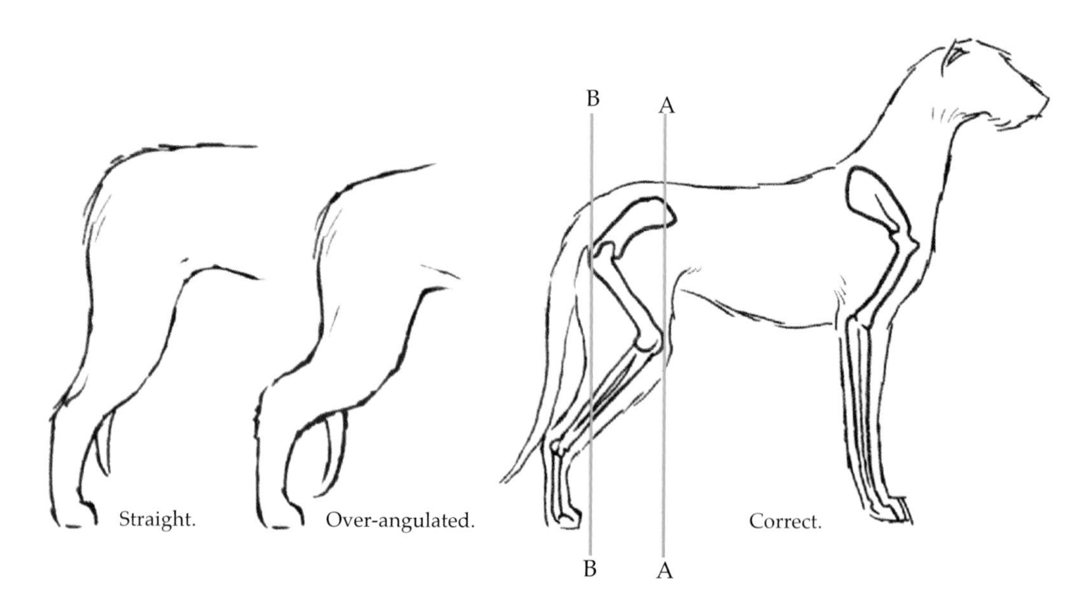

Fig 5: Hindquarter construction.

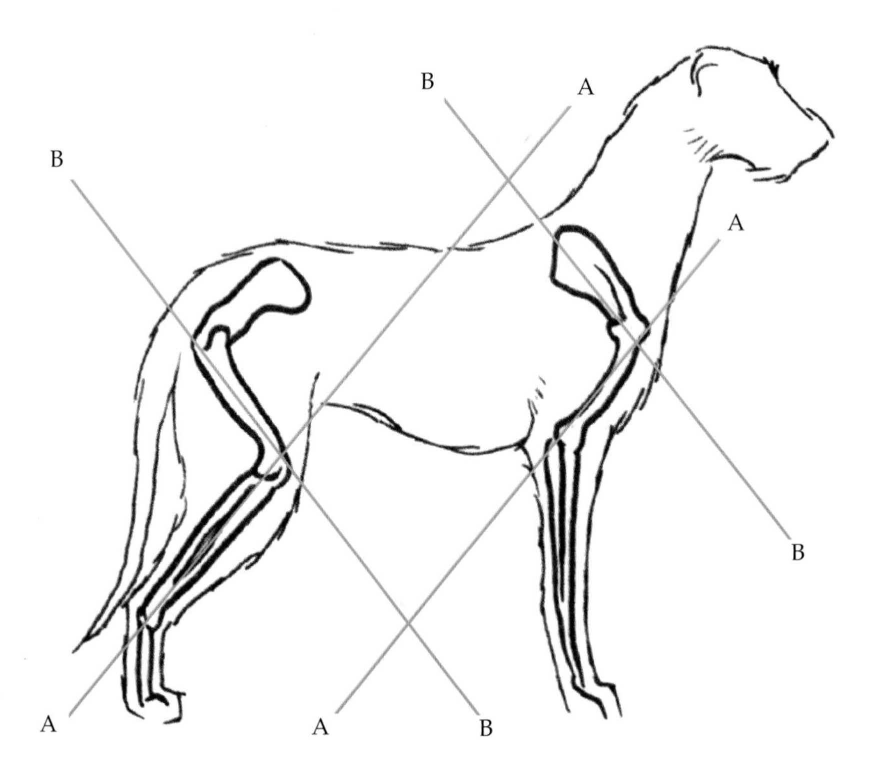

Fig 6: Forequarter and hindquarter angulation.

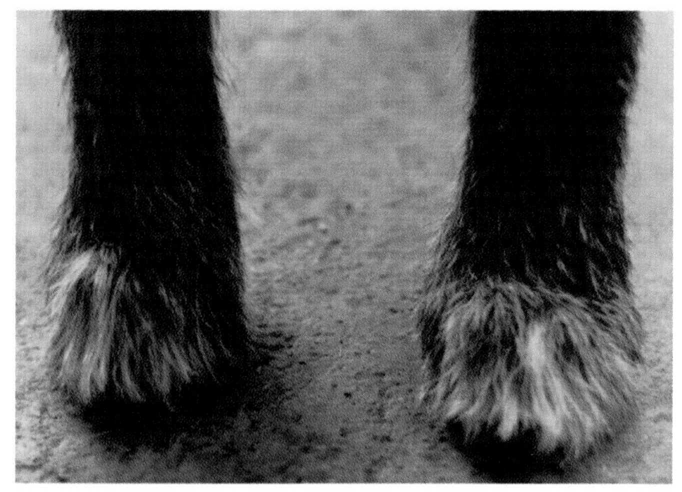

Excellent feet.

There has been a fashion in recent years for over-angulated hindquarters which are considered by many to look attractive in the show ring although, from a functional point of view, these are as undesirable as very straight hind assembly. When a Wolfhound is standing foursquare, ideally the stifle joint should be in line with the hip joint (see Fig 5 line A) and an imaginary line drawn down from the back of the buttock should fall in front of the hock to the toes of the hind foot (see Fig 5 line B).

Fore- and hindquarter angulation should be complementary. In a hound with perfect conformation, standing with hind- and forelegs parallel, the bone of the upper arm would run parallel with that of the second thigh (see Fig 6 line A) and the shoulder-blade would run parallel with the bone of the upper thigh (see Fig 6 line B). In any well-made hound these parallels conform, although the angle at which they lie will vary between individuals.

10 **Feet**: Medium sized, round, cat-like feet with arched toes tight together, strong nails, and thick pads with tough soles are essential for the hunting hound, as they absorb concussion and are less prone to injury. Flat, splayed feet put strain on the pasterns and allow damage to the skin between the toes, which is extremely difficult to treat and heal. Long, hare-like toes will break easily, as will weak nails, causing extremely painful damage to the quick or nail bed. There is a very pertinent old saying: *A greyhound finds its food in its feet.*

11 **Hair:** This is graphically described as being tough and hard, thus able to repel rain and not become entangled in undergrowth, which would be a hindrance when hunting. What is not written into the Standard of Excellence, but was said by Captain Graham, is: *His coat should be dense next his skin, and longer and more wiry on the outside. It should be a* ***double coat...*** Unfortunately, nowadays soft and over-long coats seem to have become acceptable, serving only to add glamour to the show ring.

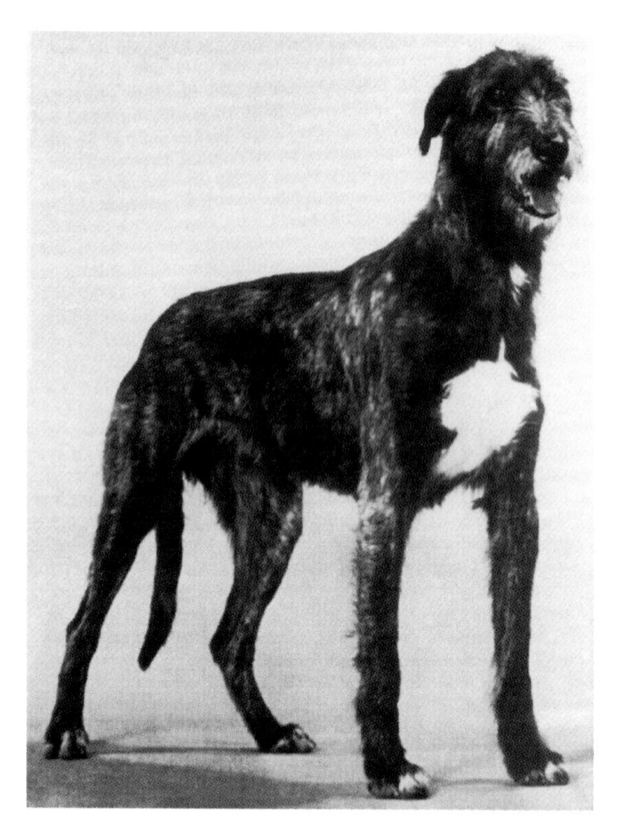

Two early Irish Wolfhounds.

12 Colour and markings: White toes, chests and tail tips are found on Wolfhounds of all colours. Some judges, totally without justification, penalise these markings, which were prevalent in many of the very old and much-admired lines. Such markings are not condemned in the Standard of Excellence. Again I quote an old adage: *a good dog can't be a bad colour.*

In conclusion, and as a reminder to those who already enjoy judging and all who aspire to judging the breed, I quote from Captain Graham's final article:

> ***... a firm stand must be made against awarding prizes to hounds that are not absolutely sound, as the breed is essentially a galloping one and meant for rough as well as fast work, and therefore coat, soundness of limb, and freedom of action, must be insisted on. Girth is also most essential, as without it, the necessary lung and heart action is impossible... It therefore behoves all Judges of this breed to see that the unsound hound never receives a place in any class, it being much better to make no award than to give a prize to a hound that may be largely used for perpetuating cripples.***

Who knows how this leggy pup will grow up?

CHAPTER FOUR

Easy rider.

OWNING AN IRISH WOLFHOUND

Most people who have known an Irish Wolfhound say they would love to have one themselves, but there is no doubt that, in purely practical terms, this is not the breed for everyone. Apart from the obvious things like size, appetite and exercise, the most important consideration is have you *time* to own one, and are you prepared for the responsibility that comes with ownership of such a large dog? This is an energetic, hunting hound who must have freedom and space for at least one long gallop every day, as well as a disciplined road walk. Also, lest you forget the strong, natural instinct that characterises a sighthound, this will be readily demonstrated, often at the most unexpected, inopportune or embarrassing moments, by the propensity to chase anything that moves! If you live an urban life this may upset neighbours with pet cats or small, nosy dogs; if you live in the countryside it can prove a worrying liability if you are surrounded by sheep or other livestock.

Good companions.

Wolfhounds and people

Apart from proper feeding and exercise, a Wolfhound's main requirement in life is to be with its owner or family. This is not a breed that can be left all day while you are at work; your Wolfhound needs to be with you, likes to 'help' with whatever you are doing and be included in everything – and will put up with discomfort or inconvenience to achieve this. It cannot be stressed too strongly how much a Wolfhound needs to be with people although, if your lifestyle necessitates leaving one regularly for short periods, a canine friend will be accepted readily as

Wolfhounds like to be with you at all times. Brona loves travelling in the sidecar.

a substitute for your company. Left entirely alone, Wolfhounds can be quite destructive once boredom sets in, or annoy the neighbourhood by 'singing' at length, loudly and mournfully.

Despite the need for their own people, Wolfhounds generally are somewhat stand-offish with total strangers and can appear quite affronted by enthusiastic over-familiarity from them, preferring to initiate quiet introductions themselves before allowing demonstrative admiration and affection.

In the home

In many ways Wolfhounds are perfect family members. They are clean in the house, shed little hair and have a seemingly natural affinity with children and an empathy with the frail or handicapped. They are extremely gentle, affectionate and sensitive to human moods, although they do go through stages of 'teenage' clumsiness and exuberance. If you are a collector of ornaments or *objets d'art* that you treasure and like to display, beware: that long tail, gently waving with love and pleasure, will clear any surface with one sweep! Occasional tables carrying valuable objects are the perfect height for this unintentional canine dusting. At rest in the home Wolfhounds take up surprisingly little room when provided with their own bed or chair and, although they cover a great deal of floor space when sprawled out, they are content to let you step over them rather than move from a comfortable position. Visitors often describe our cottage as 'carpeted with Wolfhounds': a most apt description. Once they are allowed on the furniture, you may as well resign yourself to sitting on the floor. I find it quite amusing how

GB Ch Edgecroft Simon, Top Winning Irish Wolfhound 1969–1972, shows that he's Top Family Pet as well.

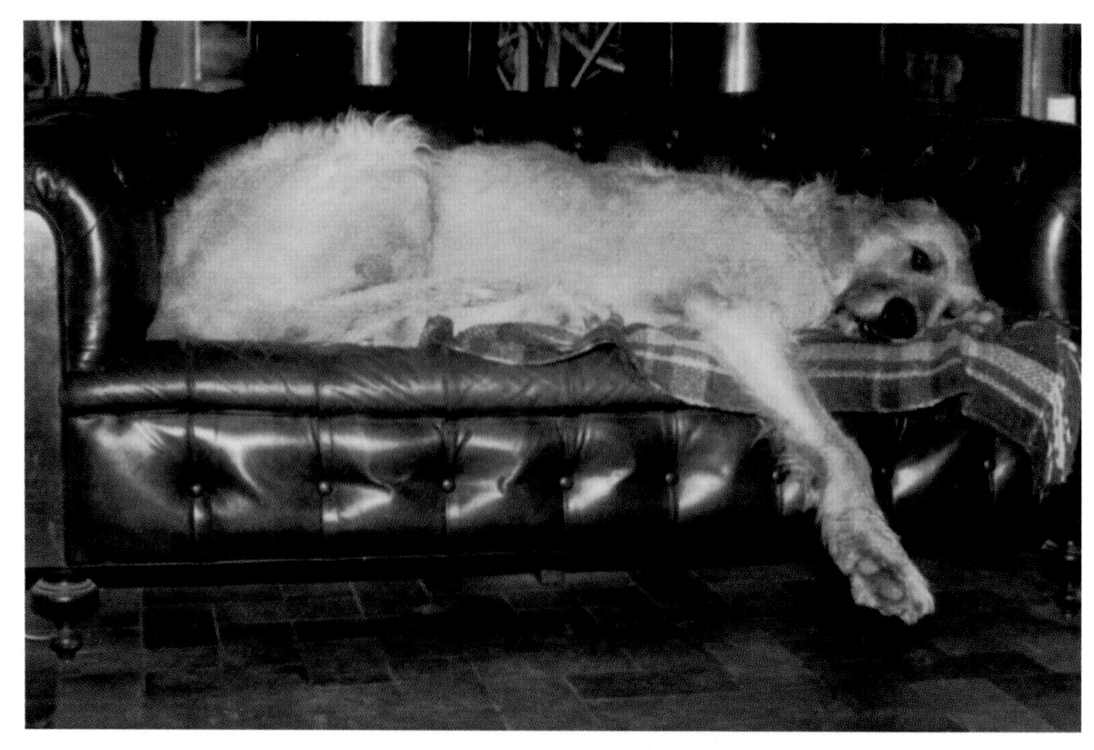

Once your Irish Wolfhound is allowed on the furniture, you may as well resign yourself to sitting on the floor.

many Wolfhound-owning friends sit there automatically in expectation of the furniture being taken over.

Wolfhounds seldom bark, so are not at all suitable as guard dogs, although the combination of their size, a hardening of the stare, raised hackles and rumble from deep in the chest will certainly make intruders wish they weren't there! Wolfhounds' extraordinarily close affinity with humans makes them acutely aware of and sensitive to ill-will or malicious intentions, and they are very accurate guides to whether anyone is a 'good' or 'bad' person. Their rôle in the family is as guardian rather than guard dog.

Dog or bitch?

Having decided you really want to own an Irish Wolfhound, the probable next question is, dog or bitch? My personal opinion (although many people disagree) is that bitches are cleverer, quicker-witted and slightly less biddable than dogs. They also come in season twice a year, which may be construed as a problem if you simply want a household pet. Dogs are usually larger, probably slightly more imposing, but just as affectionate and gentle as bitches. In my experience, they have a less independent streak, making them easier to train. On balance, there is very little to choose between them.

Adult or puppy?

If you are worried about the time and work involved in raising a puppy (detailed in Chapter 6) you may like to consider offering a home to an adult hound who has been taken in by one of the Irish Wolfhound rescue services run by most of the breed clubs. This can prove a wonderful introduction to life with this magnificent breed, and the love and devotion you will receive from such a hound makes taking in a 'rescue' extremely rewarding. Quite often hounds have to be rehomed through absolutely no fault of their own; separation or divorce, family illness, an unexpected job change and move, even sudden allergic reaction to dog hair have all necessitated parting with beloved pets. If you think you would like to share your home with an adult or needy hound, the club secretary will put you in touch with the appropriate person, but you must be prepared for an in-depth 'grilling' to ensure that you fully understand what you will be taking on, and your responsibilities. This in-depth interview is also to help the rescue service personnel match an appropriate hound with you, your family and lifestyle, ensuring as far as possible that you will all be happy together for the rest of that hound's life.

Remember that strong, healthy, nine-week-old Wolfhound puppies have a habit of growing up!

Buying a puppy

If you decide to buy a puppy but do not already have friends in the breed to consult, the club secretary or The Kennel Club will provide you with a list of breeders. Then it will be up to you to telephone or write to enquire whether they have puppies available, giving your own details and requirements and making appointments to visit where possible. Be prepared for the barrage of questions you will be asked. In fact, if you are not closely questioned as to why you want a puppy and how you intend to keep and feed it, beware: you may be considering buying from a less than conscientious breeder who seeks only to make money and will not give the support and back-up you will need during the first few months of ownership.

A 10-week-old puppy whose legs have not yet caught up with her tail.

Do not expect to be able to get a puppy immediately. Most reputable breeders have them booked in advance, so you will have to go on a waiting list. Even when puppies are immediately available, patience and discerning comparison pays dividends. In other words, do not allow yourself be won over by the first litter you see and buy on impulse; better to take time, go to several kennels and look at as many litters as you can before deciding. Always ask to see the mother of the pups (father too if he is at the same kennel) and as many close relatives as possible so that you can assess temperament and get an idea of what your puppy may grow into. Ask particularly about longevity and health, and give these aspects very serious consideration. You will pay the same price for a potentially long-lived healthy puppy as for one with the likelihood of a short life and possible congenital problems. It goes without saying that you should never consider buying a puppy that does not appear healthy, well-covered with flesh under loose, pliable skin, and with clean shiny coat, bright alert eyes, and cool damp nose with clean clear nostrils. Limbs should be strong and straight with no strange-looking bends or twists (although knees and feet should look comically large) and the tail should be long, quite thick and strong. Colour is a matter of personal preference, but usually changes to a degree as the puppy coat is replaced, so don't be at all surprised to find that you end up with a hound of different colour from that described on its registration paper!

Since the puppy has so much growing to do and patterns of development vary so greatly, no more helpful advice can be given about what to look for when choosing a puppy than to take advice from the breeder, who will be just as anxious as you are that you go home with the right puppy. In my experience, it is usually the puppy who does the choosing anyway. It is almost impossible to resist the one who continually comes to you and demands attention and affection.

If you have already done some research and think you know what breeding you would like or from which kennel you would prefer to buy, be prepared to wait quite some time before a puppy becomes available. Use that time to visit and get to know the breeder and stock so that, when there is a puppy for you, you can buy with confidence and the breeder has equal confidence in you as an owner.

A word of warning before you make your final decision about buying an Irish Wolfhound: once you have shared your life with this very special breed you will never want to be without one, and you will almost certainly find that one Wolfhound soon becomes two!

No other dog can come so close to the understanding and kindly companionship
that exists between humans as this dog can.
A giant in structure, a lamb in disposition, a lion in courage;
affectionate and intelligent, thoroughly reliable and dependable at all times,
as a companion and as a guard he is perfection.

J A McAleenan (early 20th century)

A typical Wolfhound greeting from GB Ch Eaglescrag Jake, accompanied by Juno.

CHAPTER FIVE

One of my home-bred champions, Ir Ch Owenmore Kingfisher (left), with his friend Keereen The Conqueror.

BREEDING

The decision to breed is not one to be taken lightly and without a great deal of thought and conscience-searching. The old idea that it is good for a bitch to have a litter simply is not true, and to have one litter 'just for the fun of it' is irresponsible to say the least. Can you afford to rear the puppies and have you proper homes for them? She may produce as many as 12. Equally irresponsible is breeding just to perpetuate the memory of a favourite bitch.

Anyone who harbours the notion that the responsible breeding of Wolfhounds is a profitable business is extremely ill-informed. Expenses in raising a litter may be recouped, and perhaps a little money made, if there are several puppies to be sold, no great veterinary expenses are incurred, and all puppies being sold go at 12 weeks old. If you do not have homes waiting and have to run puppies on for weeks, or possibly even months, any small profit made will be consumed – literally!

For those who love and genuinely care about Irish Wolfhounds, breeding must be with the sole aim of improving stock to the ideals demanded by the breed standard. Indiscriminate and thoughtless breeding in the recent past has resulted in a worrying deviation from original breed type, as well as a dramatic rise in health problems. Gone are the days of the large kennels of generations of carefully and selectively line-bred hounds, whose owners could predict with a great degree of accuracy the likely outcome of a mating between one of their own and a hound of almost any other bloodline. If any matings proved a genetic mismatch, manifested by poor type, temperament or health, then severe culling took place and those bloodlines were not knowingly mixed again. In more recent years the principle of selective line-breeding seems to have been disregarded, with bitches of mixed bloodlines being mated to dogs of equally mixed blood. Apart from losing a recognisable look which distinguishes one kennel from another, this indiscriminate breeding method has made it impossible to pinpoint accurately the source of any defect in conformation, temperament or health, so problems are almost impossible to correct in the next generation. Far too many people are concerned only with breeding for the show winner. Whilst such random breeding may well throw up one extremely good specimen in a varied litter, the chances of that puppy breeding consistency of type are remote. The ideal is to produce an entire litter of evenly-matched, quality, healthy puppies, all able to hold their own in conformation classes – not just one flyer.

The brood bitch

The best intentions and highest ideals of breeding are unlikely to succeed unless your proposed brood bitch is of sufficient merit. An excellent way to assess her quality and attributes is to show her. In this way you will have the opinion of several judges and the opportunity to discuss with others her merits and weaknesses, although you should first turn to her breeder for advice. She does not have

Cute Irish Wolfhound puppies grow up to be considerably taller than most people!

to be a great winner but, if she is frequently placed in large classes in the show ring, your plans for her are justified. It is best to ignore any 'helpful' person who may tell you that, although not good enough to show, she will make a good brood bitch. She may well be an excellent mother, but it will probably be an uphill and unrewarding struggle to produce quality puppies. It is much wiser to buy a good bitch from a reputable kennel if you intend to breed seriously.

Wolfhounds are slow to mature, many not having their first heat until over a year old, so it is unwise to mate a bitch before her second birthday. As a general rule, the third season is a good time for a first mating and, once a bitch is over five years old, the likelihood of fertility or whelping problems may increase, so two litters is usually the most one should expect.

The stud dog

The show ring is the shop window for potential stud dogs and many bitch owners seek the services of a dog simply because he is a champion and does well on the show circuit. Whilst this is very flattering if you are the owner of such a dog, the onus of responsible breeding rests as much on you as it does on the bitch's owner. Only if you truly believe that your dog has something to offer any particular bitch and that no faults or problems will be doubled-up on should you allow him to be used. The fact that you may receive a substantial stud fee should in no way colour your judgement. Should a poor-quality or unhealthy litter of puppies be born, you and your dog will almost certainly be held responsible. People tend to blame or praise a sire, apparently forgetting the puppies had a mother.

Breeding programme

Breeding is an art, not a science. Because bitches produce several whelps per litter, even the most knowledgeable geneticist cannot provide the formula for producing perfect puppies. Since all the physical, mental and temperamental characteristics of a puppy are derived from the combining of its parents' genes, instead of referring to *bloodlines* it would probably be more accurate to use the term *gene-line* to describe families. The secret of successful breeding is to mate two hounds whose gene combinations will result in typical, quality, healthy progeny. To this end one must learn as much as possible about the genetic make-up of the hounds concerned by studying other members of their families and any progeny they have produced. Hopefully, they will show certain characteristics in common, but much more needs to be known about each hound, with especial reference to previous generations. The more you know about these, the more accurately you can predict the probable result of your planned mating. This is where careful line-breeding is invaluable, as family likeness and traits build up through the generations.

Line-breeding: The essence of a line is consistency of recognisable type, achieved by mating together sound, typical, quality Wolfhounds of common ancestry. An affix is *not* a line – a fact of which newcomers to breeding should take very careful note, to ensure they are not misled by names on a pedigree. Many quite well-

The finished product posing for the camera.

known affix owners have no established bloodline despite years in the breed, simply adding their own affix to all bought-in hounds. A line does not come in one or two generations. It usually takes four or even five to establish and is achieved by capitalising on the virtues inherent in a pedigree, by doubling-up on and emphasising them. In general, of the two hounds to be mated, the more intensely line-bred one exerts the greater influence over the whelps.

In-breeding: The difference between line-breeding and in-breeding is not clearly defined and therefore is subject to differing interpretation. It is generally agreed, however, that in-breeding is the mating of very closely-related individuals (for example, father to daughter or brother to sister) whereas line-breeding involves mating those not quite so closely related on both sides of the pedigree. In-breeding occasionally can be extremely effective when used, *for a specific reason*, by those with deep knowledge and understanding of the genetic make-up of their hounds and previous generations in their pedigrees. It brings out recessive genes that may or may not be desirable, so could prove disastrous, especially with regard to health, if used inappropriately.

Outcrossing: Outcrossing usually implies the mating of individuals of the same breed when there is no common ancestor in the previous four or five generations although, again, this is not clearly defined. It is useful in a line-breeding programme to introduce a new point or boost a tightly-bred line. However, apart from bringing virtues you seek, it may well bring faults you did not, so it is important to return to the original line following an outcross mating.

Outcrossing can also mean mating to a different breed, usually with some similarity of type, the purpose being to alter or strengthen particular traits if a breed has become unacceptably degenerate. This type of outcrossing is rare and *only* used, as at the time of the Wolfhound revival, as part of a carefully planned programme to rebuild or redefine a breed.

Other considerations

In previous decades the main concern was to breed quality and type, little thought needing to be given to temperament or health. Unstable temperament was rare and, if one or two of a litter died, it was accepted as part of the process of natural selection, only the fit and healthy surviving. Today, however, these factors play a much greater part in evaluating breeding stock.

Veterinary science has made such progress that puppies previously non-viable are now saved, perhaps unwisely, to live an albeit shortened life. Unfortunately, too many people of insufficient knowledge, under the pretext of working for the good of the breed, insist on 'test mating' such hounds to see whether they repeat their own problems, selling on the progeny. These in turn may be bred, thus perpetuating predisposition to ill-health.

If veterinary diagnosis suggests that an inheritable trait is the cause of illness or defect, then it would better serve the future of the breed if it were assumed that all siblings could be carrying (but may not show) the same problems and to make every effort to ensure that they are never bred from. Numerically, Irish Wolfhounds are not in danger, so there is no excuse for perpetuating ill health.

It is an unfortunate fact of life that certain bloodlines just do not mix, producing either unhealthy or temperamentally unstable hounds. Shyness and any form of aggression have no place in the Wolfhound character and should be bred away from just as much as poor health or bad conformation.

The mating

Having agreed with an owner that his or her dog may be used, say when you expect your bitch in season, let the stud dog's owner know as soon as she comes in, and be sure you have agreed terms for the services of the dog. Some stud dog owners take a fee, others want first pick of a puppy from your litter; some allow only one mating, others two; some want the fee at service, others wait until the bitch is confirmed in pup or has puppies on the ground; some take the fee with a free return of service if the bitch does not conceive, others take no fee unless the bitch has a litter of a minimum specified number of puppies.

Your bitch should be in the peak of condition if she is to be bred, neither too fat nor too thin but fit and well-muscled. Before coming in season she should be wormed and her vaccinations should be checked; she may need a booster to ensure she passes maximum immunity on to her puppies. Usually the bitch is taken to the dog rather than vice versa. She will be ready between the 10th and 14th day, the 12th day often being the optimum. At this time her vulva will be swollen, her discharge will have changed from red to a very pale pink or straw colour and she will put her tail right over to one side when scratched at the root of it. She should not be given a big meal before mating, and must be allowed time to become accustomed to her surroundings and relieve herself before being introduced to the dog.

The stud dog also should be in peak condition, well exercised and fed on highly nutritious foods. He, too, should be given only a very light meal some hours prior to a mating and allowed time to relieve himself.

Wolfhounds should never be turned loose and expected to mate unsupervised, but they should be allowed time together in an enclosed area to get to know one another and play, to encourage as natural a mating as possible. Some males are extremely affectionate with the bitch, courting her gently and encouraging her by licking her ears and face as well as her hindquarters to induce her co-operation before attempting to mount. Others can be quite rough, and the bitch may need reassurance and quiet encouragement from her owner. Both hounds should have collars on and, when the bitch has allowed the dog to mount and the mating is imminent, her lead should be attached and her head held gently but securely in case she takes fright at the moment of penetration and tries to turn and bite the dog or rush forward to escape him. A sensible or experienced stud dog should not need a lead, but the collar may be necessary to take him away from the bitch

Beautiful cream hounds at a Wolfhound gathering.

should she resent his attentions. As soon as they tie, the dog should be helped off the bitch by lifting one of his front legs over her back. Then they usually stand quietly together until the tie ends.

The bitch may squeak or moan softly whilst the tie is in progress, and one extremely experienced breeder once told me that this is a sign of a good mating: a love match! Great care must be taken that neither tries to pull away from the other during the tie, as this could cause damage to one or both. The length of a tie does not affect the size of a litter and may last from 5 to 45 minutes. It is no guarantee of conception: simply definite proof that the male has ejaculated seminal fluid into the bitch. This contains millions of spermatozoa, but only as many can be used as there are ripe ova to fertilise, so it is the bitch who determines the size of the litter. Seldom is a male sterile, but if he has mated more than two bitches unproductively it may be a good idea to have his sperm tested, if only for your own peace of mind.

As soon as the mating is over, the bitch should be shut up, or put straight back in the car if you have travelled. She can be offered a drink of water, but preferably not allowed to urinate for about half an hour. Most bitches are thoroughly pleased with themselves following a good mating, and appreciate praise and love as they try to tell you all about it with big grins on their faces. My hounds live as a pack and, if a bitch has been mated at home, I find it safer to keep her away from the others for a while, just in case jealousy should start a squabble. The dog also needs to rest quietly by himself and drink a little water. Be sure he does not take too much at once, for fear of torsion after his exertions.

Occasionally a bitch will not accept the dog to whom she is taken. This is usually because she is not quite ready, although she could have set her heart on another dog, perhaps the one she usually lives with. If this is the case it may be almost impossible to persuade her to accept your choice of mate. Smears taken by a vet confirm a bitch's fertile period but, if she resents the attentions of the chosen male when he is very keen to mate her and she is definitely ready, it may be necessary to muzzle and forcibly restrain her to achieve a mating. If she really puts up a fight and plainly does not want to be mated it is as well to postpone the event; nature may be intervening to indicate a hidden problem, possibly something as simple as hormonal imbalance.

A sensible, experienced dog usually only tries to mate a bitch when she is absolutely ready, but it is not unknown for a male Wolfhound to have no interest in even the most alluring bitch. Some young dogs are over-excitable and enthusiastic, requiring some restraint and help; others do not like to be watched by strangers, forcing the bitch's owner into hiding before they get to work. Conversely, I know of one who will not mate a bitch if any member of the family is around, happily performing without inhibition before strangers.

There is seldom any real difficulty in achieving a mating, however. Needless to say, the hottest point of the day is not a good time to expect a dog to work with enthusiasm; it is better early in the day or in the cool of the evening.

Care of the pregnant bitch

Exercise should continue as normal until the bitch begins to tire more easily or shows signs of being in whelp. At this stage, avoid exercise with other hounds; too much rough play or a collision might hurt or damage her. Those who are normally very active may continue to be so until just before whelping, and they may show very little sign of being in pup until the seventh or even the eighth week if they are naturally very fit, with a tight tuck-up. More often the first signs, such as enlarging of the nipples, swollen lines along each side of the belly and a fullness through the loins or rounding of the ribs, are visible from about the fourth or fifth week. An ultrasonic scan can be taken, or the abdomen can be palpated to try to determine whether a bitch is in whelp, but neither method is accurate or infallible. Patience is certainly a virtue at such times, and the nine-week gestation period can seem forever when one is anxiously awaiting puppies.

Very little change in diet is needed for the first three or four weeks, although the bitch's meat ration may be doubled when she will take it and more milk given. It is also a good idea to give a vitamin and mineral supplement if she doesn't normally get one. High-quality protein is essential and it would be wise for those who give commercial complete foods rather than meat to upgrade to one with a higher protein content or to one specially formulated for the in-whelp bitch. Most pregnant bitches go off food for a few days or become excessively finicky; some have 'morning sickness' for a while and may take nourishing drinks instead of food. This phase soon passes and the appetite may become ravenous for a time. It is best just to accede to the bitch's demands and give her what she wants when she asks for it.

From five or six weeks onwards the bitch certainly needs extra, smaller meals, even is she does not look very full or heavy. The pups are taking up abdominal space and she may not have room to take in sufficient quantity in one or two meals. Unless she is normally very greedy or very fat, allow her as much as often as she wants. As she starts to lactate she will probably drink a great deal more than usual, so she must have unlimited access to water or milk. Milk is particularly beneficial if she will drink it as it provides the extra calcium she needs.

Whelping

Whether you whelp the bitch in the house or out in a kennel, she will need a very large bed to accommodate herself and the pups. It should be long enough for her to lie full length with room to spare, and wide enough for her to turn round comfortably. The sides should be high enough to keep out draughts. Rubber matting cut exactly to size makes an ideal base cover, as it is warm, soft and easy to wipe and disinfect. For the actual whelping it can be covered with layers of newspaper, which can be removed when soiled. When the whelping is over the newspaper can be replaced with fleecy veterinary bedding, which is warm and comforting for puppies and easily washed and dried. Take care that the bitch does not dig it up and lose a pup underneath.

An ambient temperature of about 30°C (85–90°F) is recommended for newborn puppies in their first week, with reductions of about 8–10° weekly thereafter. An infra-red lamp at a suitable height over the whelping bed will provide this heat. If pups lie on their backs away from the bitch, they are too warm and the heat should be reduced.

The bitch should be introduced to her whelping quarters at least a week before she is due so that she is accustomed to sleeping there. If left to her own devices she will quite possibly choose to dig a hole under a bush or hedge to make a nest for her babies. Even her designated quarters will be vigorously dug and tested. Most bitches have their pups on the 63rd day, but it is as well to be prepared a day or two in advance, and warn your vet. The bitch's temperature will drop from the normal 39°C (101.1°F) to below 38°C (100°F) 12 hours before whelping and she will become restless, start nesting and may go off her food, although some display a voracious appetite. Many bitches go into a deep sleep just before whelping to prepare for the coming effort.

While many advocate leaving a bitch to whelp alone, I firmly believe in staying with her – in fact my own bitches become agitated if I try to leave them as their time approaches. You should have the following items ready:

- scissors in a sterile solution in case an umbilical cord needs cutting
- some soft towels to dry and clean the whelps if the bitch cannot cope
- a heated pad or hot water bottle in a box in case one or two pups need to be distanced from the bitch while others are being delivered
- scales for weighing the newborn
- writing equipment to record details and markings
- plenty of newspaper
- plastic dustbin liner for the soiled paper
- a small bottle of brandy as emergency reviver for the bitch, pups or self!

It is also useful to have a torch (at night) and lead at hand to take the bitch out

Ten-week-old Daisy. It is impossible to know whether you have a future champion at this age.

to relieve herself during a protracted whelping. If this is necessary, also take a towel in which to catch any puppy she might inadvertently pass while urinating.

The length of time between the delivery of pups can be as long as two or even three hours. Then sometimes two come close together. One of my bitches quickly delivered five puppies and then waited 48 hours before presenting me with two more, both alive and well. However, it is wise to consult your vet if there is a delay of more than three hours in case a puppy is stuck and holding up the rest or uterine inertia has overtaken the bitch. In the latter case she may be given the hormone oxytocin to induce contractions. It is important to try to account for a placenta for each whelp and it is said to be good to allow a bitch to eat some to induce the flow of her milk. Vets sometimes like to give an antibiotic as a precaution against infection following parturition.

Once the bitch has finished whelping, her hindparts should be washed with a mild disinfectant. Offer her a drink of lukewarm milk, egg yolk and honey, and then allow her to settle quietly in the warmth to get used to her new family. Make sure that each puppy has learnt to suckle and none is being pushed out. However, if the bitch herself keeps pushing aside and rejecting one of them, you can be certain there is something wrong with it and should not make strenuous efforts to keep it going. This is nature at work. The pup may look fine physically, but is possibly brain-damaged, encephalitic or malformed internally and will not survive naturally. Trust the bitch to know best, harden your heart and concentrate your mind and energy into caring for the others. A rejected neonate is most unlikely to thrive.

If you choose not to stay with the bitch during whelping, check her at least every hour to make sure that all is well and the puppies are warm, content and suckling, cleaning up and changing bedding as necessary.

The usual number born is six to eight, but some bitches produce twelve or even fourteen and need help to rear them. With a large litter, culling (or not) should be a thoughtful decision taken for good reason. Just because a newborn pup is smaller than the rest does not mean it will always remain so. In this very large breed the smallest often ends up the largest; if it survives the first few days and can battle its way to the milk bar it should certainly not be deemed non-viable. It is equally ludicrous to suggest that any such puppy, properly reared, should never be bred because it will always produce small offspring. My own experience has proved the opposite more than once.

A healthy, well-fed bitch can usually manage to suckle up to eight puppies without help but, if she has more, it may be necessary to supplement by bottle-feeding to ensure the whelps get plenty of nourishment and the bitch is not exhausted. Be sure to use only a milk powder specially formulated for neonates, and rotate the puppies on the bitch so that each gets its share of mother's milk. If you have a very large litter it may be worth considering using a foster mother if one is available.

The bitch will need to be encouraged to eat small, very nourishing meals at frequent intervals and take lots of fluids to help her make milk until the puppies are weaned. She may not want to leave her babies so must be fed in the bed. If she is still reluctant to eat, try placing food on her legs. She will automatically clean it off, which should awaken her interest in food; then her appetite will soon return. Some bitches never go off their food, proving much less of a worry to their owners.

For the first few days you will probably need to put a lead on the bitch to get her out of the bed and away from the puppies for a short while to relieve herself and stretch her legs. It is important to make sure she gets some exercise to restore circulation and keep at bay any stiffness resulting from her lying in one position for a long time while suckling the puppies. Never take the bitch off the property or to any place where strange dogs may have been, for fear of introducing infection, easily carried on her feet or coat. Despite immunity passed on by the bitch, the puppies will be very susceptible to infection until they themselves have been fully inoculated, so very great care must be taken.

'Is it worth chasing?'

Breeding problems

False pregnancy: Just occasionally a bitch will have a false, or pseudo, pregnancy. She displays all the signs of being in whelp but, when her 'due date' arrives, her swollen tummy goes down and there are no puppies, although she is lactating. If she has a great deal of milk the vet will prescribe medication to dry her up; otherwise she would be very uncomfortable and there could be problems such as mastitis. False pregnancy can be a recurring problem and, if it distresses the bitch, some vets advise spaying.

Reabsorption: There have been many cases when a bitch who, when scanned, has been found in whelp produces nothing, or who has initially given every indication of being pregnant for several weeks only for all the signs and symptoms to disappear spontaneously. These are indications that the bitch may have reabsorbed embryos. Research has shown that this problem can be caused by faulty production of progesterone. A deficiency of this naturally-occurring hormone is one reason why a pregnancy cannot be sustained. Tests can be taken by a vet regularly throughout the pregnancy to determine hormone levels, and any deficiencies can then be redressed.

BHS: When breeders ask for swabs to be taken before a mating, these come from the terminal vagina which, in normal healthy bitches, has a resident population of bacteria including, among others, some *Beta haemolytic streptococci (BHS)*. If there have been problems getting a bitch in whelp, this can sometimes be because an excessive burden of BHS has affected sperm deposited. An infection of the uterus sufficient to affect fertility would not be detected by vaginal swabs so, if this is suspected, more searching tests should be made before further matings.

Thyroid problems: Thyroid problems can affect a bitch's fertility. A blood test will show any deficiencies.

CHAPTER SIX

An alert, four-month-old pup.

FROM BIRTH TO MATURITY

Rearing the litter

In the first few days following birth, the most important thing is to ensure that all the whelps are feeding well and the bitch is taking care when moving. Until their eyes are fully open there is a danger of the puppies being squashed. Some bitches are extremely careful and even appear to count the pups and put them all together before getting into or out of the bed; others are very careless, so the owners' vigilance is needed to ensure survival.

Healthy, thriving puppies are fairly quiet, though an occasional yelp or grunt may be heard and a great deal of twitching will be observed. Constant noise, mewing or complaining sounds indicate discomfort: the puppies may be too hot, too cold, hungry or unwell. Watch carefully to see that each one defecates but, if any yellowish-coloured diarrhoea is passed, consult your veterinary surgeon at once. If any are constipated or have passed nothing within 12 hours, administer two or three drops of liquid paraffin with an eye-dropper.

When the puppies are four days old the dewclaws should be professionally removed as they can can get caught or torn as the pups grow up and become more active. They also spoil the look of the front legs in a show dog. Wolfhounds usually only have dewclaws on the front legs; if they have dewclaws on the hindlegs too these should definitely come off. The nails should be clipped or filed regularly as they are surprisingly sharp and could scratch the dam, causing bleeding and great discomfort.

At ten to twelve days the eyes will start to open – always an exciting event. By now the pups are up on wobbly legs and staggering about. Soon after the eyes have fully opened you can feel teeth beginning to erupt, signalling that the digestive system is ready for something more solid than just milk, so it is time to start helping the bitch with the feeding. Every breeder has his or her own methods of weaning and rearing, but the important thing is that puppies get the very best of everything. The body weight almost doubles weekly so to reach their full potential they must be given plenty of top quality food. Many scientifically-formulated complete foods are available for puppies and dogs of all ages and stages of growth, and many people rear Wolfhounds entirely on these. Their use certainly ensures that basic nutritional requirements are met. However, I am of the firm belief that, as dogs are carnivores, they should be given plenty of meat at all stages of their development, so my own rearing methods may well be considered old-fashioned.

The next few weeks can be a frighteningly expensive time; appetites increase rapidly and astonishing amounts of food are consumed. Nevertheless, an old adage says that the first 12 weeks of a puppy's life are the most important in establishing health and resistance patterns that will affect the rest of its life, so it is an unwise and false economy to be sparing with either quality or quantity of food.

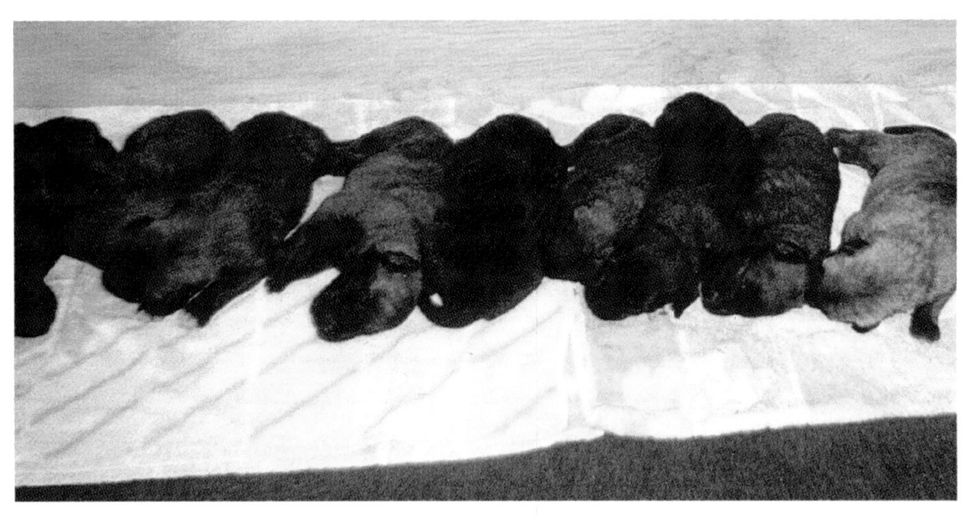

A litter of eight-day-old puppies.

I begin weaning with two meals a day, feeding each puppy individually on raw, scraped beefsteak in the morning (about a walnut-sized piece is sufficient for the first day or two) and a meal of a proprietary brand of baby cereal, made up to a runny consistency as directed on the packet, later in the day. My rule is to give each pup as much as it wants at each meal, feeding individually for at least a week – they are, of course, still suckling. When they are all eating well they share a communal dish, but are watched to see they each get a fair share. From four weeks old, progress is rapid and they need four or five meals a day, with mother's milk

The same litter at five weeks.

as well. The meat is now finely minced and fed twice daily, they have whole-wheat cereal with warm milk and honey and I introduce a complete, commercially manufactured puppy feed for one of their meals. Their feeding dish is raised slightly so that they can eat without reaching down, and this also discourages them from walking through the food. They enjoy a drink of fresh, clean water and it takes some ingenuity to devise a firm stand to prevent the water bowl being constantly up-ended.

Puppies are born carrying roundworms and from four weeks need to be wormed regularly as prescribed by your vet. It is important to watch carefully from 12 hours after dosing and clean up any worms passed.

The bitch must be able to leave the puppies at will and, if they are all eating well, she soon has them weaned and happily drinking fresh full-cream milk or reconstituted, high-fat-content powdered milk as a replacement for hers. Fat-reduced and semi-skimmed milk are not rich enough to supply the energy needed by these fast-growing youngsters, and it is essential that all puppies have plenty of milk daily to cover their calcium requirement. Other dairy products such as plain yoghurt, cheese and eggs are also good for them. Whole eggs should be cooked, as raw egg white in quantity can cause a deficiency of the vitamin biotin, causing loss of hair, dermatitis and poor growth. Raw egg yolks are highly nutritious and much enjoyed, especially when beaten into a little oil. At this stage I add a liquid vitamin and mineral supplement to their cereal meals and offer finely-chopped, cooked tripe, alternating with red meat. At about six weeks they get their first raw bones to chew. Marrow- or knuckle-bones are best, and now is the time to teach them to give these up on demand without fuss and not to squabble with their litter-mates.

A seven-month old showing width and strength in hindquarters and hocks.

Whether to supplement feeding with added calcium in the form of bone-meal is subject to debate, much depending on the basic diet given. It has been shown that over-supplementation can cause more problems than a less-than-perfect diet. Each Wolfhound puppy is genetically programmed to reach a certain size with a particular amount of bone, no matter how poorly or well it is fed. A good diet merely ensures that this potential is fully reached without undue stress or illness. No amount of bonemeal or added calcium gives the hound bigger bones or makes it grow taller, and any excess may lodge in joints and cause damage. It is not the lighter-boned hounds who benefit from or need extra calcium, but the very heavy-boned puppies may well require more than the basic diet can provide to ensure strong, straight growth of their long bones and prevent stress fractures or bowing of the legs. When feeding bonemeal, this should be counterbalanced with extra vitamins A and D to aid absorption and utilisation and is easily given in the form of halibut or cod liver oil.

A nine-week-old bitch from Owenmore.

Like much to do with dogs, good feeding and rearing are matters of common sense and close observation. A diet containing plenty of quality meat, wholemeal biscuit, cereal, cooked and raw vegetables, milk, some eggs

Two nine-week-olds enjoying a tug o' war.

National pride – Irish Wolfhounds greeting foreign visitors.

and occasionally tinned sardines or fresh fish (carefully boned), supplemented when necessary by daily treats of vitamin and mineral tablets such as Canoval, has proved an excellent diet for many years. The advent of complete, commercial feeds has simplified meal times, but it is my personal belief that nothing is so good for a hound as an adequate supply of quality meat to utilise properly and satisfy the digestive system and help build strong, elastic muscle. I find the commercial feeds tend to go through a hound's system too quickly and do not appear to satisfy for long. It is rather like eating a Chinese meal yourself – delicious and very healthy, but hunger pangs return all too quickly! The other difficulty when relying solely on complete foods is that you cannot make minor adjustments to fat, protein or carbohydrate levels to cater for individual requirements. When rearing puppies, it is essential not to use the very high protein puppy meal beyond 12 weeks, as it can push growth unnaturally fast, inviting problems.

Young puppies need plenty of attention and to be handled and played with. It is surprising how early character develops. They must have freedom to run about, explore and take what exercise they need but, as they will follow you for miles, it is best just to sit and watch their games develop. They must be free to stop and start at will as too much, or forced, exercise can strain joints and limbs. If they have to be left without human company for any length of time it is good to leave a radio on softly. This seems to comfort and relax them and they get used to strange noises.

All puppies must be inoculated and your vet will advise when best to do this – usually at 8 and 10 weeks, or 10 and 12 weeks, depending on the vaccine used. If a puppy is being sent abroad it is wise to check well in advance what vaccinations are needed, as requirements vary between countries.

Puppies should not go to their new homes until they are 12 weeks old, although 10 weeks is perfectly acceptable if they are going to experienced owners. If they are allowed to go any earlier they will not have had a complete course of vaccinations, nor will they have built up much strength or resistance to disease and infection. In males, both testicles may not have descended, so cryptorchidism can go undetected. Until about 10 weeks they are still reliant on mother as guide and mentor. If they are going abroad, airlines will not transport them before before they are 12 weeks old. Letting puppies go at 7 or 8 weeks will certainly save their breeder a great deal of expense, but it may prove costly to the new owner. A Wolfhound puppy can prove an expensive and heartbreaking investment if there are problems early on, so it is well worth waiting the extra week or two insisted on by more caring breeders.

The new puppy

No matter how many years you have been in the breed, the arrival of a new puppy is always an eagerly-anticipated event and, if you are a first-time owner, it can be very nerve-wracking until you fall into a routine of feeding, exercising and rest and learn to stop worrying about your pup's progress. Your greatest ally is the breeder, who will not mind how often you ring up to seek advice or ask apparently inane questions. Wolfhound puppies are usually very adaptable, laid-back creatures, accepting new situations readily and adjusting quickly to new surroundings and routines. However, they are also adept at using their appeal to great effect in persuading you to do their bidding, making it plain that *they* are inviting *you* to share their lives, not vice versa. For this reason, it is important to ensure that your new puppy knows and responds to its name, and to establish a routine and some house rules.

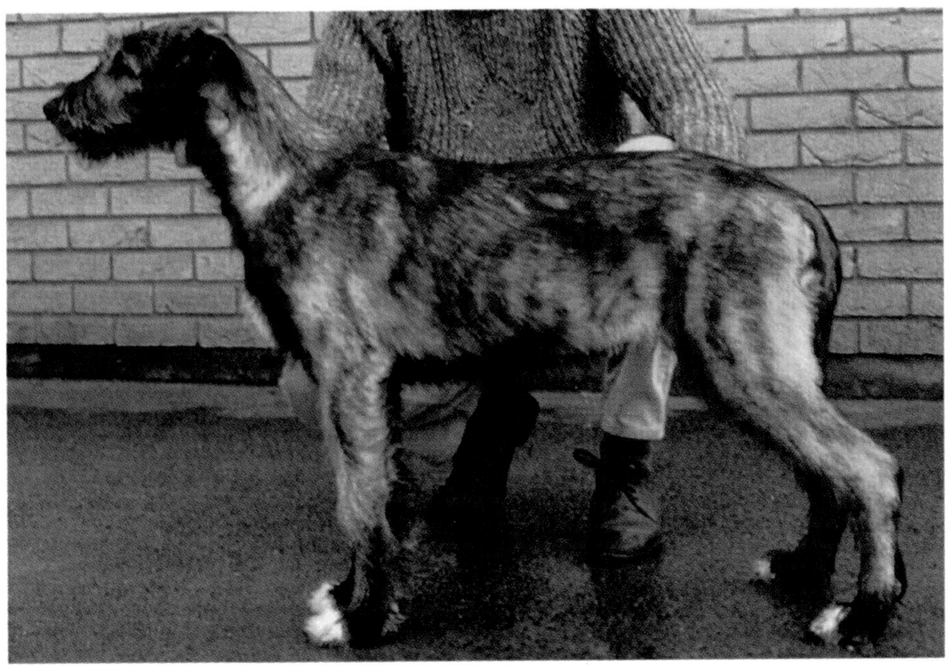

Int Ch Culvercroft Benjamin of Gulliagh at four months.

Int Ch Culvercroft Benjamin of Gulliagh, aged two.

The greatest cause of anxiety to new owners occurs when puppy will not eat the amount expected and rejects everything so carefully itemised on the diet sheet provided. Now is the time to be firm and not allow yourself to be panicked either into offering a selection of tasty treats or, worse still, hand feeding. No puppy will starve itself for more than a day or two at most. By weakening and giving a choice of meals you set a pattern that is extremely hard to break.

The feeding area should be a quiet place with no distractions. Prepare a meal from the diet sheet and stay with puppy while it eats. If you put down food and walk away puppy will be anxious to be with you and ignore the food. Allow your pup about 20 minutes to eat and, if it refuses or stops eating, take away the food until the next scheduled meal, when you repeat the process. If you have allowed it to drink a quantity of milk immediately before a feed do not be at all surprised that it won't eat: milk is a food and very filling. Treat the milk as a meal, but do not be tempted to substitute it frequently for solid food. If puppy goes through a few days of refusing food, vitamin and mineral tablets posted down its throat ensure it does not want for nutrients.

Wolfhounds should always have their food bowl raised off the floor, allowing them to stand straight and eat at a comfortable height. As they drink a surprising amount of water, a bucket is usually a better receptacle than a bowl, but be sure to wash it out and provide clean water every day.

Int Ch Culvercroft Benjamin of Gulliagh at five-and-a-half.

The other major worry for new owners is the question of exercise, too little being as detrimental as too much. Again, common sense must rule. Freedom for your young Wolfhound to play at its own pace in a large, safely-enclosed area is the ideal, preferably with you, its owner, or an equally-matched canine friend. As you watch, you will soon recognise when your dog is getting tired. You should then take it to its bed and leave it to sleep undisturbed for as long as it wishes. As soon as your puppy wakes up, take it out to relieve itself before offering a meal.

Once your puppy is completely at home and confident in its surroundings, it is time to start lead training. Most puppies can be trained easily and quickly by a system of praise and reward, their greatest desire being to please and gain a cuddle. However, lead training is sometimes a little worrying in that puppy may resent being caught, feel trapped and rear up or pull away, or else sit firmly on its behind and refuse to budge. These are perfectly natural reactions, so reassure your pup and make a fuss of it when it stops resisting, or hold a favourite titbit far enough away to make it get up and reach out for it. When the puppy is on its feet and relaxed, allow the lead to go slack and play with it and offer titbits, encouraging it to go along with you. Soon the pup will think this a good game and forget about the lead. Keep each lesson short, but repeat it twice a day. In no time at all the pup will be happy to be 'attached' to you. After a week or so, start teaching it to walk quietly beside you without pulling off in all directions. Some young Wolfhounds are extremely strong and wilful and may need one or two sharp checks with a check-chain to encourage them to stop tugging against you. This is a lesson which must be taught before puppy becomes big and strong enough to take you off your feet. An alternative method of lead training is given in Chapter 11 under **Heel**.

The daily routine should include time for a little grooming for, although a good coat does not require much attention, a daily brush keeps the skin in good condition and removes any dead hair, as well as preventing the build-up of fleas or other parasites. Grooming and trimming are detailed in Chapter 7.

Growing up

As the weeks go by and puppy gets stronger, playtime will be longer and sleep-time shorter and puppy will be looking for mischief. Like children, some pups are more destructive than others, but firm, gentle admonishment should soon teach what is allowed and what is not. Usually, a severe tone of voice is sufficient, or the pointing finger with a very firm *No*. The ultimate punishment for persistent and defiant wrong-doing can be a light smack with a rolled-up newspaper, the noise giving a fright, rather than the blow hurting. *Never* smack a Wolfhound with your hand: hands are for praise and love, not punishment.

Once your puppy is fully lead trained and confident you can take it out for short walks and introduce it to the neighbourhood. It is important to work at socialising a young hound, especially if you intend to show, and the more accustomed that hound becomes to different places and situations the better. When walking it on a lead you will need to adjust your pace to suit the puppy, as long, gangling legs and big bones make pups very uncoordinated and it can be difficult for them to find a comfortable speed on a lead. As well as a short daily road walk, the young Wolfhound needs space for a good gallop to stretch its legs and muscles. However, it should not be allowed to race with adult hounds, as they will be too fast and may knock it over.

Feeding

From six months to about eighteen months old a young Wolfhound generally needs four meals a day, including at least 1.4–1.8kg (3–4lb) meat. Fresh green tripe is ideal, and it is very beneficial to give half a kilo of liver once a week. The largest meal should be given late in the evening so that the dog goes to bed with a satisfied stomach, digesting the meal while resting. From eighteen months on, three meals a day are usually sufficient. One can be just milk and cereal with an egg yolk and honey beaten into it. From two years of age, a meal morning and night, with milk offered during the day, is ample. Wolfhounds should be fed twice a day throughout their lives, two slightly smaller meals being preferable to one large, as their stomachs are relatively small. They are not usually greedy, so the rule should be to give as much food as is asked for at each meal, meat being given every day.

Most hounds enjoy a slight change of diet, and well-cooked pasta, rice or pearl barley makes a good alternative to biscuit or cereal. Any scraps from your own table added to the usual meal are appreciated, and the dripping from a roasting tin is a special favourite. Lumps of suet make a wholesome treat and, in winter, a teaspoon of cod liver oil daily helps to ensure a healthy skin and coat. Marrow- or knuckle-bones keep teeth and gums clean and healthy.

This seven-month-old bitch puppy from Killykeen already shows strong, muscular neck and strong, straight bone.

Nutritional requirements

The nutritional needs of a very fit and active Wolfhound (or any sighthound) differ from other breeds in that, when they run and chase, sudden and tremendous amounts of energy are required in short bursts, ideally followed by a rapid recovery time. Most breeds expend energy at a lower level over a longer time and need to be fed accordingly.

Proteins are the 'building blocks' of the body, providing for growth, formation of muscle, and repairing any wear and tear. Together with the amino acids, of which they are composed in differing levels and combinations, proteins determine the hound's potential for speed and recovery, which is why a feeding regime should include protein from more than one source, the main ones being meat, poultry, eggs, milk and fish.

Fats provide energy, and all sighthounds have higher fat requirements than most other breeds, although individual metabolisms will determine the rate at which fat is converted so needs will vary with each hound. Fat is also essential for the maintenance of skin and coat condition. Sources include vegetable and corn oils, animal fats such as suet or dripping, and the fish oils, which are particularly rich so possibly best restricted in summer or hot climates.

Carbohydrates provide the starches and sugars that help proteins and fats to be used efficiently and are mostly found in cereals and grains, which should always be cooked, and rice, pasta and potatoes. Insufficient carbohydrate in a diet causes protein to be used for energy, leaving less for tissue repair and growth.

Vitamins and minerals should be adequately supplied by a natural diet so, once adulthood is reached, supplementation is unnecessary. If you are feeding your hounds entirely on commercially-manufactured complete food it is important *not* to supplement, for fear of upsetting the balance.

Water is a vital part of diet, and Wolfhounds drink copiously at all times of the year. It is essential in processing and eliminating from the body the waste products caused by digestion or hard running, so it is important to ensure that water is of high quality, uncontaminated, and preferably free from too much chlorine and other chemicals. If you are travelling between countries with a hound it is wise to carry a supply of water from home; a change upsets the stomach just as much as a drastic alteration in diet. If a hound has been subjected to long periods in the heat, it is a good idea to put electrolyte replacer in the water to alleviate stress or potential dehydration.

The advisability of continual and exclusive use of commercially-produced complete foods for the Irish Wolfhound, or any giant breed, is currently being called into question by many senior breeders and owners, who are worried that digestive, fertility, skin and temperament problems may be aggravated by an undiluted 'unnatural' diet. *Dogs are carnivores*, so their digestive system has evolved to deal with meat, sinews, fibre and bone. Although these ingredients make up the commercial feeds, they are processed to such a degree that the dogs' very strong natural digestive juices become almost redundant. It is interesting that, as far back as the late 1800s, Mr Mahony (Dromore strain), commenting on size deterioration in the breed, thought that, when people's diet changed radically from meat to mainly vegetables in the 15th century because of the decline of the deer population, not only did the big dogs prove costly to keep, but their size suffered because there was little red meat to preserve it. He said this adversely affected their power and speed and brought about a decline.

Because it could lead to torsion or bloat, never feed a Wolfhound fresh from exercise, still panting and with a racing heart; nor should it be allowed drink much whilst in this state. It is said that a puppy cannot bloat, but I don't think it's worth the risk. For the same reason, fast or energetic exercise should not be allowed for at least an hour after a meal, although pottering about quietly is fine. This rule should be adhered to throughout a Wolfhound's life as bloat and torsion, although by no means always caused by the above, are unbelievably distressing for hound and owner, frequently fatal or causing permanent damage.

Rate of growth

Between six months and eighteen months, the young hound (especially if it is going to be very big) may go through short periods of sudden and rapid growth. At such times exercise must be curtailed, and the hound should be left in peace and quiet to rest and sleep. Extra milk and a vitamin/mineral supplement should be given and, if food is rejected, small, favourite nutritious morsels offered.

Occasionally, during a growth burst, joints may feel warm or even slightly swollen. An adult dose of paracetamol relieves pain and lowers any slight temperature at such times. This usually only lasts three or four days, after which your hound will be back to normal, although exercise should be restricted for a further week to allow joints and bones to settle again. If ever a joint really swells or is obviously painful it should be checked at once by your vet. Any significant rise in temperature, unexplained inactivity or reluctance to exercise should also be checked professionally as soon as possible.

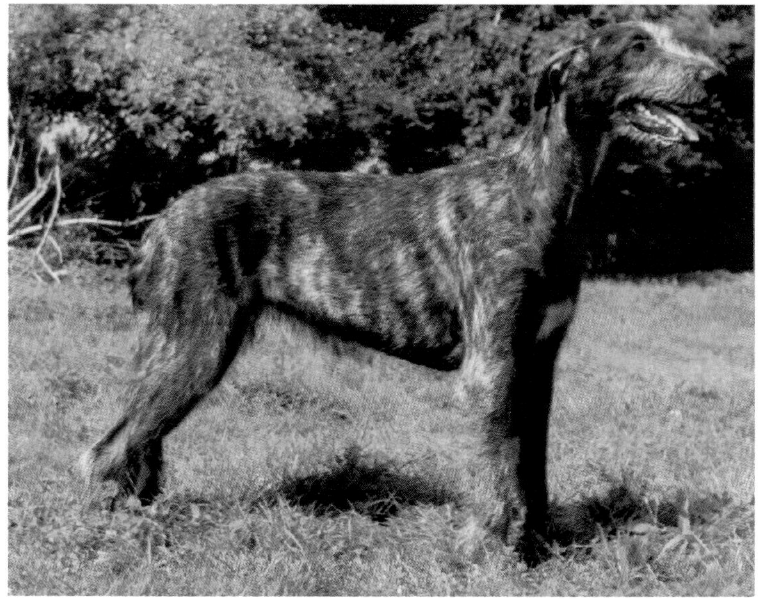

Ir Ch Owenmore Kestrel at thirteen months (below) and five-and-a-half years (above).

'Ears take on a life of their own.'

Wolfhounds tend to grow unevenly, rather like young horses – high in the loins and croup one week, then higher in front with a slope off behind the next. Backs seem to lengthen and shorten and heads change a great deal both in shape and size, movement goes through very erratic stages, and there are times when ears take on a life of their own. Great patience and total faith in the breeder who assures you that this awkward, uncoordinated juvenile will turn into a creature of grace and nobility are essentials for anyone owned by this breed. Take comfort in the fact that the most beautiful, balanced, coordinated puppies who win so much seldom go on to do well as adults, while the less attractive puppies frequently fulfil very early promise and mature into top-class hounds.

Some hounds think they're pups for a long time – Owenmore Finn Mac Cool at nine-and-a-half.

I am often asked how to tell when a youngster has stopped growing. A simple answer is that, once the knees feel completely flat and those huge knobbles of bone have disappeared, it has probably stopped growing up, but may take at least another year or 18 months to body-up and fully mature. A good male is unlikely to be at his best before four years old.

Young Wolfhounds also frequently go through a stage of being 'precious' and a little shy. If this happens, do not be over-protective or allow them to run away or cower behind you. This only reinforces timidity and is nearly impossible to correct later. The best policy is to ignore them when they are being silly and pathetic. They soon miss the lack of attention and affection. If they want to lean on you or hide behind you, keep moving away to make it impossible. If you react firmly and positively to situations that cause your hounds anxiety, they soon gain reassurance from your attitude and the phase will pass. The sensitivity of this breed to the moods and reactions of an owner should not be underestimated but used to advantage to raise a happy, well-adjusted and confident Wolfhound. There is a great deal of truth in the saying that there are no bad dogs – only bad owners.

The old hound

Unfortunately, Wolfhounds do not live to a great age. Most of their lifetime is spent growing up, with a relatively short period of maturity before a fairly rapid decline into old age. Nowadays, nine is considered a very good age for a hound, ten years and over being exceptional, and with present-day health-related problems and (dare I suggest?) unnatural feeding methods, the expected lifespan is currently about seven-and-a-half years. Some bloodlines seem to live longer than others, but no difference has been found between dogs and bitches. I believe we underestimate how much stress contributes to shortening a hound's life, incessant travel and showing constituting the greatest strain. If we wish to prolong our hounds' lives it behoves us to try to eliminate the stress factor, beginning in puppyhood.

No single factor predisposes a hound to die early, although degeneration of the heart can be expected in most elderly hounds. A weakening heart can be easily regulated by daily medication prescribed by the vet, and a mild diuretic may also be necessary to prevent fluid build-up. Life can certainly be prolonged by keeping an elderly Wolfhound as active as possible, on an easily-digestible and highly nutritious diet, with a warm, draught-free, extra-thick, soft bed and plenty of tender loving care. It is important to ensure that your senior citizen gets plenty of your time and attention, and preferably has a gentle friend for company. Interest in life and the family must be fostered and, even if stiffness and a certain reluctance to move sets in, your hound should be encouraged to take at least one daily stroll or, if it is regarded as a treat, a ride in the car. Allowing the older hound to become a 'couch potato' and eat too many fattening treats will not help, and its routine should be maintained for as long as possible. Having a puppy in the house will interest the old hound, who may even decide to educate the newcomer.

Galtymore Pride of Keerleen, still strong and shapely at ten-and-a-half..

A daily grooming with a brush keeps skin and coat in good condition and the hound will enjoy the massage. Weekly attention must be given to ears and teeth to ensure they are kept clean and healthy. Nails grow long faster with less road walking, so may need to be cut more frequently.

Apart from adjusting diet, it is a good idea to give a daily dose of Evening Primrose or Starflower oil (gamma linoleic acid), which alleviates and helps to prevent some of the stiffness of arthritis or rheumatism. Cod liver or halibut liver oil is good too, but more needs be given. I have also found that the wonderful elixir known as Anima-Strath, or Bio-Strath, the human but identical version, keeps the entire system in excellent order. This is a Swiss-made mixture of yeasts, herbs, fruit extracts and honey in a very palatable and easily-digestible form. Honey is an excellent food, very easily assimilated, and is said to increase resistance to infection and help to relieve the aches and pains of old age. A tablespoonful daily in a little warm milk and cereal is much appreciated.

Elderly hounds who take very little exercise can fall prey to pneumonia, so any sign of wheezing, coughing or increased respiratory rate should be checked by the vet. If your hound is just a little thick in the lungs a herbal expectorant will ease the problem. I have found that antibiotics, despite curing some specific ailments, can affect old hounds adversely, leaving them depressed. Herbal treatments seem to work more gently and in harmony with the system.

Killykeen Jermyma, still mistress of all she surveys at eleven-and-a-half.

During hot weather, or after a course of antibiotics, there may be a tendency to dehydration, possibly owing to a reluctance to get up to take water. This can be remedied by syringing adequate amounts of electrolyte with glucose drinks into the side of the mouth at frequent intervals.

If soreness and stiffening of the limbs afflict the old hound, you must be aware of the times when it is likely to want to relieve itself, and make every effort to help it to its feet and outside. Even if your hound is reluctant to move, firmness must be used; it is important that the bowels and bladder are kept working regularly, and examination of faeces and urine gives a good indication of state of health. Wolfhounds are naturally very clean dogs and are absolutely mortified, suffering desperate embarrassment, if they soil their beds.

It is always to be hoped that a beloved hound will pass away peacefully and naturally but, if the time comes when your elderly friend can no longer get up at all, or is in obvious distress, the humane and courageous decision must be made to have it put gently to sleep. Nothing is more unkind to a Wolfhound than to allow it to endure loss of pride and dignity.

CHAPTER SEVEN

Friends.

GROOMING

All dogs enjoy the individual attention of daily grooming, none more so than the Wolfhound, although it is not strictly necessary for this breed if the coat is of correct length and texture. The purpose of regular grooming is to remove dirt, debris and dead hair and to stimulate the skin to produce the natural oils that offer protection from the weather and make the coat gleam when the hound is in good health. The close contact also affords the ideal opportunity to check for parasites, small wounds, abrasions or loss of condition. If you cannot give even a cursory brush every day, spend more time on a thorough grooming twice a week.

GB Ch Erindale Clarion of Finloren perfectly groomed for the show ring.

You will need a fairly stiff bristle brush and a comb with well-spaced teeth, although a fine wire-toothed slicker brush or hound glove is particularly good for grooming a rather soft, long coat. Careful attention should be given to the hair on the face and the beard, where any knots should be very gently teased out with the comb. Then a vigorous brushing all over the body and legs keeps the coat tidy and in good condition, doubling as a massage and promoting hair growth. The tail also must be brushed or combed, with regular inspections of the hair under the root of the tail and around the anus, where it often becomes matted or soiled. If it has, it should be cut short, neatly and carefully. This is one of the very few areas where scissors can be used on a Wolfhound, the others being around the feet, between the pads, on the elbows and around the sheath of a male. These areas are rather sensitive, so plucking the hair by hand could hurt.

An Irish Wolfhound head in need of trimming.

The same dog after trimming.

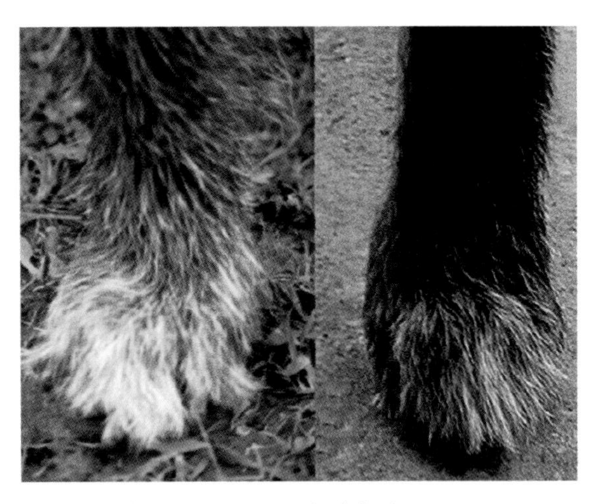

(Left) before trimming, (right) after trimming.

A little hand-stripping is necessary to enhance the appearance of your hound and have it looking its very best, particularly if you intend to show. To do this, take a few hairs between finger and thumb and tug sharply in the direction of growth. You will find it comes out quite easily and, with practice, your wrist stops aching and it soon becomes second nature. Beginning at the head, pluck all the long hair off the ears. Underneath you will find very short hair with a velvety texture. Once you are down to this the ears will look smaller and neater: an instant improvement and encouragement to go on! Long hair frequently sprouts, Mohican-fashion, on top of the head and can also become profuse on the cheeks so, taking care to leave eyebrows and beard intact, pluck and tidy these areas too. Removing the thick ridge of hair that invariably grows on either side of the neck enhances its length, and any untidy tufts on the topline along the back, or over-long hair hanging from the stomach, should also be removed to accentuate the hound shape. The hair at the base of the tail often grows rather thick and bushy, so this should be plucked just sufficiently to blend with and continue the smooth line from the croup. Please never scissor or razor the tuck-up to try to accentuate it, even if your hound is a shade portly – it merely looks ridiculous and unnatural.

Tufts sprouting from the elbows should be trimmed carefully with thinning scissors and, if there is a thick growth of hair on the knees, this should be plucked to make the knees look flatter and prevent the appearance of being knuckled-over. Long hair around the feet also needs trimming to enhance their neat shape and discourage any build-up of mud and dirt.

Particular care should be taken when tidying a hound for show not to overdo stripping and trimming. This can give an unnatural appearance to what is, after all, a rugged hunting breed. How much tidying is necessary varies considerably between individuals, depending on the quality and texture of the coat.

At some time during the year your hound may take on a rather 'moth-eaten' appearance and get itchy as it tries to shed its coat. When this happens you will find that hair comes out incredibly easily and in quite large tufts so, to speed up the process and encourage the growth of a new coat, it is a good idea to pluck your hound out all over – right down to its underwear! For a couple of weeks your hound will look somewhat under-dressed and may even feel a little sheepish for a day or two, but it will feel better for the drastic treatment and a lovely new coat will soon come in. Don't be at all surprised to find the new coat a shade darker than the previous one or, in the case of creams, richer.

If your Wolfhound has a rather soft long coat (incorrect but prevalent), regular and conscientious work on it can improve the texture greatly. Daily combing to rake out soft undercoat makes it easier to pluck the longer top hair and, particularly in grey and brindle hounds, the new hair is coarser. Never be tempted to cut long coats with scissors or thinning shears. It does nothing for the texture; using clippers simply ensures that the coat will grow back thicker and softer than ever.

Unlike most of the short-coated scenthounds such as Bassets, Beagles and Foxhounds, which are notorious for exuding a distinctive 'houndy' smell, Wolfhounds have little personal odour, so seldom need bathing for deodorising purposes. Twice a year is usually sufficient, unless you feel it necessary for a special show. If you are bathing a hound with this in mind, do be sure to do so as much as a week beforehand. This should give time for some of the natural oils to return, so that the coat settles down and loses the fluffy texture caused by most shampoos.

It is never too soon to encourage good coat growth. As they appear, the very long, sparse 'cat hairs' characteristic of a young puppy should be plucked out. This must be done frequently. Removing these helps the proper puppy coat to come in evenly. Puppies enjoy the attention and it gets them used to being hand-stripped from a very early age.

Checking inside the ears for signs of mites and canker should be part of the daily grooming routine. If a dark, waxy substance is present, cotton wool moistened with very dilute hydrogen peroxide can be used to clean the ear flap and gently into the ear canal. Application of any readily-available anti-parasitic eardrops alleviates the problem but, if it is persistent, seek veterinary advice.

Nails should be inspected regularly and clipped when necessary. Although it helps, road walking is not guaranteed to keep them short enough or of even length. Dewclaws, if present, certainly need frequent attention and regular clipping. Good quality, sharp clippers should be used, and the nail cut as near to the quick as possible without causing bleeding. If the nail is white it is easy to judge how far back to cut, as the pink flesh inside the nail can be seen clearly. Black nails are more difficult to gauge, but close inspection of the underside reveals that the extra nail is a thinner layer, probably slightly hooked and extending beyond the solid area housing the quick. If in doubt, take just a little cut at first, then file the nail down. With practice you will get to know how much to remove. If you draw blood by cutting into the quick, don't worry. It may take a long time to stop bleeding, but no permanent damage will have been done, other than making your hound wary of having its nails cut again. A good way to stop the bleeding is to dip a little cottonwool into Stockholm tar and stick it to the nail. Not only is the tar antiseptic, but it will form a crust on the nail tip and stop blood escaping. If the nails are not very long, filing rather than clipping may be sufficient to keep them short and level.

Large knuckle bones on which to gnaw are the natural and best tools to keep your hound's teeth and gums clean and in good order, but it is advisable to check occasionally for signs of decay (especially in older hounds) and to ensure no teeth are cracked. An alternative to bones is to provide dog toys specially designed to remove tartar and keep teeth clean as they are played with. Nylabone produces a good range of these. If bones are never provided, the best way to keep your hound's teeth in good order is by brushing about once a fortnight or as their condition demands, using a stiff toothbrush and one of the many canine toothpastes readily available. Unless the teeth are cleaned regularly there is likely to be quite a heavy build-up of plaque and tartar, which must be removed by the vet or (very carefully) by you with the appropriate tool.

It takes only a few minutes each day to check over your Wolfhound thoroughly and keep it looking its best. Your hound will thoroughly appreciate the very personal and individual attention, and you will find it relaxing and therapeutic – a daily habit well worth cultivating.

A bone helps to keep teeth and gums healthy.

CHAPTER EIGHT

The picture of health: GB Ch Owenmore Blanchfleur.

HEALTH CARE

If your puppy is strong, well bred, has had the very best of feeding, care and attention for the first 12 weeks of life and is free of hereditary problems then, with continued loving care, annual booster injections, regular worming and ordinary luck, it will enjoy a healthy and trouble-free life.

Irish Wolfhounds are basically a healthy breed. However, there is a trend for too many breeders to persist in breeding from bitches who are proven carriers of hereditary problems or stud dogs known to have passed on genetic defects. This has given the breed a somewhat 'unhealthy' reputation. Anyone contemplating buying a puppy should check its pedigree very carefully and seek advice from several well-established and respected breeders before committing themselves to the expensive purchase of a puppy who may carry the potential for health problems. Not only is it extremely distressing living with a seriously unwell Wolfhound but the correct treatment can be very expensive; so why buy potential trouble? Patience and research can ensure you get a puppy from a kennel of healthy stock, and that is well worth waiting for.

Irish Wolfhounds are 'silent sufferers', seldom complaining or giving obvious signs of pain or distress, so it is very important to know your hound and its daily habits and behaviour patterns, a deviation from which is often the first indication that something may be wrong. In my experience the eyes are the greatest pointer to how a hound is feeling. Any loss of shine and sparkle indicates discomfort and, if they are positively dull or the third eyelid is showing, there is probably something more seriously wrong. A dry nose sometimes indicates a raised temperature, as do very hot ears, but marked changes in behaviour patterns are the strongest indicators and should never be ignored. In most cases there is nothing wrong and normal behaviour is resumed quite quickly. Watch your dog carefully while you are trying to ascertain the problem and, if there is no sign of improvement after a few hours, seek veterinary advice – it is always better to be safe than sorry. Many veterinary surgeons will tell you that rules for other breeds do not necessarily apply to Wolfhounds; just occasionally, a hound can become very seriously ill quite suddenly, with little or no warning.

Should it ever become necessary for your hound to have any sort of operation, it is important to be aware that Wolfhounds are very susceptible to anaesthetic, requiring a great deal less than might be expected for their size and weight. Most vets are well aware of this and modern drugs are very safe but, if your veterinary practice seldom deals with giant breeds, a tactful reminder may be in order.

A rectal thermometer is an essential in your first aid box. A dog's normal temperature is 38.3–38.6°C (101–101.5°F). It is a good idea to know and note your hound's normal pulse rate, which will be between 70 and 100 beats per minute. The easiest way to count the pulse is by using the femoral artery located inside the upper thigh. A raised temperature, say 39.4°C (103°F), or increased pulse rate requires veterinary advice.

The more natural curative properties of homeopathy may be of interest to owners who worry about the side or after effects of drugs used in conventional veterinary medicine. The following section is written by Mr George Kinsella, a practising veterinary surgeon highly qualified in both homeopathic and conventional medicine, and is intended as an introduction to this very effective and natural method of treating problems and illness.

Canine homeopathy

Treatment of dogs with homeopathic remedies is very safe and has **no** side effects. In many instances the remedies work quickly and very effectively but, even if there is little or no response, at least one can feel confident that no harm is being done. This cannot be said for conventional orthodox medicine, where steroids and antibiotics can harm the patient.

Homeopathic treatment works by stimulating the immune system, not by suppressing it, as conventional treatment does. This strengthens the body's own power of healing – the *vital force* within the patient.

Homeopathic remedies increase the production of interferon, which inhibits the development of viruses. They also increase the body's resistance to infection. Samuel Hahnemann discovered by a chance observation that Peruvian Bark (Cinchona or 'China' – active principle: Quinine) could produce signs and symptoms in a healthy body (his own) quite indistinguishable from those of malaria, a disease it was singularly well able to cure. This apparent paradoxical effect he named *Homeopathy.* The Greek word *omios* means *similar,* and *pathos* means *suffering* – hence *similar to the suffering,* the treatment of a disease with a substance that produces the same signs and symptoms as those displayed by the ill patient.

Unlike conventional medicine where one applies *the law of opposites* (for instance, giving anti-itch creams such as steroids to cure an itch), homeopathy applies the *law of similars.* In addition to this startling discovery, Hahnemann found that if he serially diluted and successed (shook violently) his curative substances at each stage they were less able to produce any harmful effects and, paradoxically, became more and more powerful curatively – the so-called *minimal dose.* We call these dilutions *potencies.* The most commonly-used potency in veterinary homeopathy is 6c (the remedy diluted 1:100 six times). This is the best potency for pathological treatment, for example, muscle injuries, bone fractures, liver disorders, and ligament or tendon injuries. In treating a long-standing chronic disease or a psychological condition such as aggression, high potencies (200c, 1m or 10m) will be necessary to effect a cure. Here we are talking about a permanent cure, not a temporary one. This usually involves treating the dog as an *energetic whole,* including not only signs and symptoms of a disease but build, character, behaviour, and personality. This is the basis of good holistic medicine.

Thus treating a dog homeopathically complies with three main principles:

- The selection of a substance (the remedy) to cure a disease knowing that the same substance could cause signs and symptoms in a healthy patient similar to those seen in the sick patient.

- By extreme dilution and succession the medicine's curative properties are enhanced and all the poisonous/toxic effects are lost.
- The prescription of a remedy takes into account the *whole* patient, according to basic temperament, build and character, not just the name of a disease.

Soft tablets are the most convenient form in which to administer homeopathic remedies internally, but they can also be given orally in liquid form or injected subcutaneously. Remedies can also be applied locally in the form of creams or lotions to wounds, cuts and muscle injuries.

Generally, remedies for acute diseases are given in low potency (6c) frequently and for chronic diseases in higher potencies, less frequently but for longer periods. The higher the potency the deeper the remedy acts and the longer it lasts.

Tablets/remedies must be stored in tightly-capped brown bottles away from strong odours and light in a cool, dry place (not the refrigerator). Tablets should be crushed to powder and placed on the dog's tongue or given to the dog on something bland such as a biscuit or piece of bread. They can also be be dissolved in water for the dog to drink. Food should not be given 20 minutes before or after administering homeopathic remedies as they are absorbed from the mucous membranes of the mouth and intestines. It is also important to try to avoid concurrent conventional treatments of steroids, antihistamines or anything that will lower the immune response.

Homeopathic remedies and all their properties are listed in a book called *Materia Medica*. For first-aid use, here is a list of the major acute remedies that every dog owner interested in homeopathy should have:

Aconite (monkshood): For sudden shock or fever, especially from the ill effects of chilling, sudden profuse haemorrhage or stress. Can be used for almost any infectious disease at the early initial stage: for example, acute parvovirus, canine distemper, hepatitis, leptospirosis and respiratory infections. Use a high potency (30c or higher). Aconite is particularly good at calming down an uptight or anxious hound before an important show: use 1m potency.

Apis mellificia (honey bee venom): For fluid swellings that respond to cool water bathing, such as bites, urtica, oedema, joint swellings. Swellings usually 'pit' on pressure. This is especially useful for acute allergic reaction to bee stings.

Argentum nitricum: This is very useful for hounds that have a fear of being handled (especially by men): give one dose daily for up to 10 days before show.

Arnica (montana plant): The great injury remedy. Can be used confidently and as early as possible in any case of shock, bruising and haemorrhage or any injury to legs or haematomas. (Classic example: road traffic accident.)

Arsenicum album (arsenic trioxide): For cases of acute vomiting and diarrhoea (try aconite first) like parvovirus or gastroenteritis, especially when the dog has a dry mouth and seeks heat. If the mouth is wet and drooling, *mercurious corr* is more appropriate. Arsenicum album is also good for acute allergic reactions, asthmatic type problems and eczema, especially where allergens are suspected.

Nutsdown dogs enjoying a romp. Photograph by Robert Smith.

Brrr! This is cold! A Nutsdown dog enjoys the water. Photograph by Robert Smith.

Bryonia (wild bryony hops): Use where movement aggravates the condition. In many cases, such as pneumonia, arthritis and acute strains, the hound prefers to lie down and keep still so that it does not aggravate the problem.

Hepar sulphuris (calcium sulphide): The 'antibiotic' of homeopathy. Use in all cases of sepsis or cellulitis. In low potency (6c) it promotes suppuration (for example, if an old bite wound needs bringing to a head) but in high potency (30c–200c) it suppresses suppuration (for example, a fresh bite wound). It helps wounds heal better and quicker than with conventional antibiotics. Combine with use of Calendula/Hypericum lotion diluted 1–20 in water and applied as a spray to the wound.

Hypericum (St John's wort): The great pain remedy. For any injury to nerve tissue, especially painful wounds, bites and where terminal portions of the body, like feet or tails, are involved. Can be used internally in tablet form or applied as a cream or lotion. Hypericum/Calendula greatly reduces licking and pain, including after spay and castration operations.

Ledum (Marsh tea/wild rosemary): Great puncture wound remedy. Has anti-tetanus properties.

Rhus toxicodendron (poison ivy): Muscle injury remedy. Relieves stiffness, especially where there is improvement with exercise, then worsening after rest. Use 6c or 1m potency.

Ruta graveolens (rue bitterwort): For ligament, tendon and joint capsule problems. Aids the healing of any fibrous structure. Most useful potency 200c, given twice weekly for four to six weeks.

Silicea: Chronic suppuration remedy, including for foreign bodies. Great for problem anal glands or sore and sensitive ears. Particularly useful if you cannot find the foreign body, such as a splinter of glass. Silicea also boosts the immune system and is an excellent pick-me-up, particularly following debilitating viral illness or severe infection. Potency 200c, given twice weekly for four to six weeks works well.

Symphytum (comfrey): The knit-bone remedy. For all fractures, especially non-union fractures of the radius/ulna, and similar.

Urtica urens (ordinary stinging nettle): For oedematous swellings that are ameliorated by warm water application. Also good for acute allergic conditions like bee stings or insect bites. A good potency is 30c. It also has a diuretic effect when used in low potency (6c).

Worming

In an ideal situation, faeces samples should be taken regularly to the vet for examination and analysis to establish how many and what type of worms your hound is harbouring before any worming treatment is administered. This is particularly important in countries where there is a danger of picking up dangerous and life-threatening parasites. In Ireland and England, where we are usually only concerned with roundworms and tapeworms, most owners routinely administer worming doses to adult hounds either once or twice a year without recourse to the vet, as various very safe and effective treatments can be purchased in pet shops or veterinary chemists without prescription.

To keep worms to a minimum and discourage them from reproducing in the hound's system, give garlic regularly, either as crushed cloves or in powdered form. This has long been acknowledged as very effective, as has the use of certain homeopathic remedies. However, these must not be regarded as worming treatments, as their very nature prevents them from killing even worms. The most effective combination is cina, kamala and granatum, and their routine use throughout the year, with one annual chemical worming, should keep your hound free of infestation.

Common problems and injuries

Many common and minor problems can be easily treated yourself, either conventionally or homeopathically, but if at all in doubt consult a vet without delay.

Cuts and wounds: Because of Wolfhounds' rough coats it is not always easy to see a cut or wound, but attention is usually drawn to a sore place by constant licking. Bathing with a mild disinfectant, followed by application of an antiseptic or homeopathic cream usually suffices but, if it is a puncture wound, it is wise to apply a warm poultice for 12 to 24 hours to ensure any infection is drawn out and stop the puncture from closing too rapidly. Although tiny, puncture wounds can be the most dangerous and need careful watching. Bruising of a tendon or ligament may have taken place if another dog's tooth caused the puncture, and the poultice will relieve any resultant swelling.

Damaged tails: This can be a nightmare with hounds, who constantly wag their tails and hit them on concrete walls or other hard surfaces, causing the ends to split and bleed. In severe cases wounds can become gangrenous, necessitating removal of the infected joints. This is a real problem that must be tackled at the first sign of blood and damage. In simplistic terms, the cure lies in protecting the end of the tail while leaving it open to the air to promote healing, hardening of the damaged skin and hair regrowth. The trick is to persuade the hound to leave the protection alone.

Having cleaned the wound and applied antiseptic ointment, wound powder or spray, my solution is to leave it unbandaged and apply a short length of tubular foam pipe-lagging towards the end of the tail to provide protection and a cushion, leaving the end exposed to the air. The tubular foam can be held firmly in place further up the tail with a strip of adhesive bandage to stick it to the hair. I have found the foam tube works better than cardboard or plastic rolls because it is very light and flexible, and spraying it with a commercially-produced anti-chewing solution usually ensures it is left alone. Unfortunately, tail damage is a recurrent problem, but in time a callous forms over the wounded area and it is much less prone to bleeding.

Comparison with a donkey shows just how much an Irish Wolfhound can grow.

Skin irritations: Unfortunately there are plenty of possible causes of constant scratching or nibbling, but the most common is infestation by **fleas**, **grass mites** or **lice**: all parasites easily dealt with by applying an appropriate spray or powder. Having treated the hound, it is vital to remember also to treat bedding, carpets and any dust-collecting area such as skirting boards and under radiators. Affected hounds frequently bite at a patch near the base of the tail or just a few centimetres down the tail, and an application of benzyl benzoate to these areas cools the skin and kills any mites, although it must not be applied to cut or broken skin. Homeopathic sulphur 30c makes the body less attractive to ectoparasites such as fleas and mange mites and should be given internally once weekly as a preventative. This is a much safer alternative to the monthly chemical doses currently widely advertised.

If bald patches appear or self-mutilation and frantic scratching persist veterinary advice should be sought in case it is **mange**.

The presence of **ear mites** is characterised by an accumulation of a black waxy substance in the ear canal and on the ear flaps, possibly accompanied by head shaking or rubbing. Gentle cleaning with cotton wool moistened with a weak solution of hydrogen peroxide, followed by administration of antiparasitic eardrops for several days, solves the problem.

Biting at the feet is indicative of **harvest mite** infestation, usually occurring in late summer and autumn and visible as bright orange dots between the toes and up the legs. Bathing with an antiparasitic shampoo is curative.

Fortunately, **ticks** pose no great threat in Great Britain and Ireland, merely attaching themselves to the skin long enough to feed and then dropping off. They are a minor irritation and sometimes leave a tiny lump for a day or two. If they are seen they can be removed by grasping the body with tweezers and turning gently anti-clockwise to 'unscrew' the burrowing head. If they are simply tugged out the head will be left behind and an infection may occur. A very heavy infestation by ticks could cause anaemia, and in many countries unpleasant tick-borne diseases are prevalent.

Too rich a diet, especially during hot weather, can overheat the blood and cause **hot spots** on the skin. Having adjusted the diet by lowering protein and fat levels, you can

Rest after play. Photograph by Robert Smith.

give relief by applying a cooling lotion such as calamine or dosing the hound weekly with a 30c potency of sulphur.

If none of the preceding is found to be the cause of troublesome skin, it may be necessary to ask your vet to test for allergies.

Bursa on the elbow: A swelling is caused when the normally empty sac lying between the skin and elbow bone becomes filled with fluid as a result of trauma, usually from lying on hard surfaces or a young hound throwing himself to the ground. Placing soft bedding, such as a foam mattress or thick carpet, in the hound's favourite resting place may help, as will affixing some form of padding to the elbow.

Bursas in puppies and young hounds can also be caused simply by the concussion created by galloping and jumping around on hard ground or too much trotting on pavements or tarmacadam surfaces; severe overweight also exacerbates the condition. Usually these swellings disappear with time and rest from concussive exercise. Massage helps disperse the fluid, as does iodine gently scrubbed into the swelling with a toothbrush.

If bursas become very enlarged, some vets like to drain them, but this invariably needs doing several times and there is always a danger of infection. The most drastic treatment is to remove the bursa by operation.

Lameness: If a hound is lame for no obvious reason, the very first area to check is the feet. If a foreign body such as a shard of glass or thorn has been picked up it is very difficult to locate. More frequently the hair between the pads traps a small stone or lumps of mud or snow. This can be helped by clipping out excessive hair.

The nail-bed is another site that can cause great pain if damaged, so the nails should be carefully checked and not allowed to remain very dirty, or particles of mud may get into this area and set up an infection.

Once the feet have been eliminated as the cause of lameness, each leg should be inspected for heat or swelling, and joints gently manipulated to try to elicit a pain response. If nothing at all can be found, the hound must be rested totally for a few hours, by which time either it will be better or further examination will reveal the pain source and treatment can be decided upon. When there is heat on a bone or joint, an ice-pack brings relief, and hopefully 12 hours' rest will promote full recovery without recourse to a vet. If, however, a joint swells, professional advice should be sought in case there is serious damage or infection. If a muscle is very tense and seems to be the cause of the problem, then the application of heat and gentle massage helps. In both cases, an adult dose of aspirin or paracetamol eases the pain and reduces any slight temperature, but be sure not to administer any analgesic containing codeine. If a hound shows great pain or the lameness is severe, seek veterinary attention at once.

Pyometra: Occasionally vaginal bacteria travel forward into the uterus and, if its lining has reduced resistance, as is often the case with older bitches, the life-threatening condition of pyometra develops. It starts during oestrus when the cervix is open, allowing bacteria to enter. After ovulation the cervix closes, the pus builds up and the bitch becomes progressively ill, with loss of appetite, increased thirst and vomiting. The condition can be difficult to diagnose unless the cervix opens slightly and allows some of the pus to escape. Veterinary attention must be sought, as intravenous fluids will be necessary. As a simple preventative measure, one 200c dose of Sepia should be given to all bitches after whelping.

Bloat and torsion: This is a very serious condition in which gases trapped in the stomach continue to expand, causing great distension with probable rotation of the stomach (torsion). *Immediate veterinary attention is essential* if the hound is to recover. Clinical signs most frequently appear some time after a meal: abdominal distension, excessive salivation and frequent but unproductive attempts to vomit, sometimes with a little foam expelled. There is very obvious and distressing evidence of pain and shock. If a hound is treated before there is complete torsion of the stomach there is a good chance of recovery but, if torsion has taken place, surgery will be necessary – although shock and interrupted blood flow may lessen the chances of survival. A hound with this frightening condition may live for up to 36 hours after onset or may die very quickly. Any sign of distension of the stomach should be taken very seriously and veterinary attention sought immediately.

To help prevent bloat, feed your hound twice a day rather than giving it one very large meal and restrict exercise for an hour before and at least an hour after feeding. However, there is evidence to suggest that a temporary metabolic disorder, bacterial activity or even a very low-grade infection may be responsible for many cases, while many gut bacteria can also produce 'gas' as a by-product, thereby worsening the condition.

Inherited diseases prevalent in Wolfhounds

Osteochondritis Dissecans (OCD): A growth-related condition that usually affects the shoulder joints but can also affect the elbow, stifle and hock joints of large and giant breeds. It is a disturbance of the maturing cartilage of the affected joint and occurs when the head of the bone and cartilage are deprived of essential nutrients. The cartilage thickens, is less able to withstand the normal weight-bearing forces imposed on it, becomes necrotic and breaks away from the bone, either as a flap or an osteochondral fragment consisting of bone as well as cartilage. This intrudes into the joint cavity, which becomes inflamed, causing pain and lameness. It is frequently bilateral, but occasionally lameness is evident in only one joint.

Causes	Inherited. Can be accelerated by mineral over-supplementation. Trauma (for instance, excessive exercising of puppies).
Signs	Intermittent or persistent limping from the affected limb. Lameness worse after exercise and stiffness and pain on rising. This condition usually appears between the ages of four and nine months, with males affected more often than females.
Diagnosis	X-ray.
Treatment	Complete rest for four to six weeks. If no improvement, surgery.
Homeopathy	Must be constitutional, but symptomatic treatment helps. In

general calcarea carbonica (calc carb) is excellent for big, bony placid young dogs. Calcarea phosphorica (calc phos) and rhus toxicodendron may also be useful.

Prognosis Outlook excellent. Full recovery within six to eight weeks of surgery. It is strongly recommended that, even when treated successfully, dogs affected with OCD should not be part of a breeding programme.

Hip Dysplasia (HD): A developmental condition resulting in abnormal looseness or laxity affecting one or both hip joints. All puppies are born with normal hip joints but some time after two weeks of age the femoral head of a dysplastic puppy fails to sit firmly in the acetabulum (socket) and the joint becomes unstable. As a result the joint capsule is stretched, the ligament that holds the head of the femur in the socket also stretches and the articular cartilage becomes eroded. In an effort to re-establish stability, new bone develops around the margins of the femoral head, neck and acetabulum. The rate of development of this new osteoarthritic bone depends on the individual puppy and environmental factors.

Causes Inherited. Rapid weight gain in puppies. Trauma such as excessive exercise or rough play.

Signs Reduced exercise tolerance. Mild to crippling lameness. Reluctance to sit or rise from a lying position. 'Bunny-hopping' gait, getting worse with exercise. Stiffness after rest. Sometimes a clicking sound can be heard from the hip joint.

Diagnosis Physical examination supported by X-ray under general anaesthesia to enable correct positioning of hip joints.

Treatment Depends on individual dog and severity and stage of condition. Young puppies may respond to limited exercise, strict maintenance of correct body weight and anti-arthritic or analgesic drugs to provide temporary relief. This treatment may allow the hip joints to stabilise by 15 to 18 months. Puppies with severe dysplasia are best treated surgically with the appropriate technique. Total hip replacement is available at almost prohibitive cost. Clinically affected stock should not be bred from.

Homeopathy Chamomilla or colocynthis greatly reduces hip pain. Symptomatic treatments include rhus toxicodendron; bryonia; calc phos; causticum; colchicum.

Un-united anconeal process: The anconeal process is part of the ulna bone. Un-united anconeal process is a fusion defect of the elbow joint, which results in constant movement of the joint, causing it to be unstable. The condition can be unilateral or bilateral, and the age of onset is usually five to seven months.

Causes Inherited. Metabolic abnormalities such as hormone imbalance.

Signs Pain, lameness, fluid-type swellings on side of elbow joint. Limited movement of elbow joint.

Diagnosis X-ray.

Treatment Surgical removal of the anconeal process.
Homeopathy Constitutional remedies such as calc carb; calc phos; lycopodium. Symptomatic remedy is symphytum.
Prognosis Good, although lameness may persist and arthritis will almost certainly occur. Treated dogs should not be part of a breeding programme.

Cardiomyopathy: Heart muscle disease occurring in the absence of any other known disease or abnormality of function. Cardiomyopathy takes more than one form, the most common in Wolfhounds being dilated cardiomyopathy, when the heart chambers become enlarged but the muscle walls are too thin and weak to pump the blood. Dilation of the left atrium frequently leads to rhythm abnormality.
Causes Inherited. Viral infections. Metabolic diseases.
Signs Lack of exercise tolerance. Shortness of breath. Fluid retention. Heart murmurs.
Treatment Drug therapy as symptoms occur.
Homeopathy Crataegus oxycantha is useful for enlarged hearts. Where there is a full but intermittent pulse and the hound does not want to exercise, convallaria majalis Q or lx potency. Strophanthus Hispidus Q or lx potency helps to slow the heart where there is a fast, thready pulse: it strengthens the beat and aids urine output in acute cases.
Prognosis Poor. Survival time between six and twelve months from onset of treatment. Affected hounds should not be bred from.

Portosystemic shunt (liver shunt): Congenital abnormality of the portal vein, causing it to by-pass the liver. The function of the portal vein is to carry blood containing absorbed foodstuffs from the intestine to the liver for processing and de-toxifying. The cleansed blood then returns to the heart via the major vein (posterior vena cava). Blood 'shunted' past the liver by a defective portal vein retains high levels of ammonia and toxins, so the entire system is slowly poisoned.
Causes Inherited.
Signs Evident in very young puppies: loss of appetite, vomiting, poor growth and development, mental disturbances including convulsions, walking in circles, disorientation. Head pressing is very common, as is seeing imaginary objects and making a grab for them. Occasionally symptoms do not appear until the puppy is a few months old.
Diagnosis Test for ammonia levels and bile acids – angiogram dye test.
Treatment Surgery. Where surgical correction is not possible low protein diet can help control build-up of ammonia.
Homeopathy Symptomatic treatments include organ (liver) specific remedies such as nux vomica, lycopodium and berberis.
Prognosis Poor; even after surgery quality of life will diminish. Lifespan shortened. Affected stock should not be bred from.

Von Willebrand's disease: Hereditary defect of platelets, leading to bleeding disorders involving the clotting process.

Cause Inherited.

Signs Excessive or prolonged bleeding following trauma or surgery. Nosebleed or bleeding from the gums.

Treatment Following a bleeding episode, administration of fresh blood or plasma.

Homeopathy Arnica; phosphorus; silicea; and most of the 'snake venom' remedies like vipera (adder) and crotalus (rattlesnake).

Progressive Retinal Atrophy (PRA): This describes a number of inherited retinal degenerations. In all cases vision is severely affected and blindness may result.

Cause Inherited.

Signs In some cases, night blindness. In daylight pupil dilates widely, giving staring expression. In poor light conditions the hound may bump into objects.

Treatment None.

Homeopathy Phosphorus – a great general eye remedy. Use 30c dose for 21 days, but there is often need to use in ascending potency. In such cases use 200c twice weekly for one month then 10m twice weekly for a month.

Bone cancer: Although this does not come into the category of proven inherited disease, it *is* prevalent in the breed, occurring more frequently in some bloodlines than others, so it is wise to avoid breeding such lines together.

Signs First signs are pain and lameness, with or without localised swelling, and any unexplained lump on a bone needs to be monitored carefully. Fractures may occur through the weakened area. Lameness is progressive as bone is destroyed.

Diagnosis X-ray used to confirm diagnosis.

Treatment Many cases can be treated with radiotherapy or chemotherapy, but this may only prove palliative. Amputation is an option as this effectively removes the tumour and associated pain. Bone cancers frequently lead to secondaries in the lungs.

Homeopathy Silicea 200c is very good for bone cancers. Hecla lava can also be used, especially if the head bones are involved.

Prognosis Depends on the individual.

Mammary cancer: Always check bitches carefully for lumps on the mammary glands, particularly after they have whelped.

Treatment Always consider surgery, which may be the first choice treatment in many cases.

Homeopathy For early small ones use conium maculatum (hemlock) 30c, then use in ascending potency. If they are just soft mammary swellings use phytolacca (poke root), and if they appear after a false pregnancy use pulsatilla 200c.

Irish Wolfhound clubs around the world are conducting health surveys, carrying out research into and exchanging information regarding inherited diseases but, if the instances of hereditary defect and disease are to be minimised or eliminated, the onus is upon the owners to shoulder the responsibility of *very* selective breeding and ensure that known or likely carriers are *never* used. This applies equally to stud dogs and brood bitches. This breeding strategy will inevitably involve heartbreaking decisions, but it is the ultimate answer if the vitality and viability of the breed are to be stabilised and improved.

Owenmore Goshawk and Owenmore Osprey at nine weeks.
Continued good feeding and appropriate exercise will ensure they maximise growth potential.

CHAPTER NINE

Aus Ch Greyhavens Holly aged three-and-a-half years with Sue Lewington.

SHOWING

If your ambition is to make a name for yourself in the world of dog showing, and Group and Best in Show (BIS) wins are a cherished dream, an Irish Wolfhound is probably not for you. Unlike the more exuberant and glamorous breeds, where sheer showmanship and skilled grooming can catch the judge's eye and may sometimes elevate a mediocre specimen to great wins, the Wolfhound, with its quiet dignity and relaxed movement, relies almost entirely on a judge's appreciation of breed quality and soundness for high placement in Groups.

Pendomers Water Colour receiving an award.

As a breed the Irish Wolfhound is not a natural showman and few genuinely enjoy the experience, especially at indoor, benched shows. A lack of enthusiasm and cooperation and the difficulty of moving a very large dog in the confines of a frequently-too-small ring can cause the handler great frustration and the hound a surprising amount of stress. It often requires great patience and empathy to persuade a Wolfhound to give of its best in the ring, and each owner must put the well-being of the hound first in deciding whether to show. An unhappy hound will never do itself justice and, for the sake of lasting health and longevity, the stress factor should be given very serious consideration.

Having presented the negative aspect for new or prospective owners to whom a career in the show ring may be of major importance, let me follow with the rider that, if it is not the winning but the taking part that appeals and your hound enjoys the outings, you will certainly find showing great fun. You meet and make friends with people of like interests, and much can be learnt about the breed by

BIS: Int Ch Hydebeck Reginald Snuffson (left), Reserve BIS: Ch Owenmore Cinniuint (right).

attending shows and talking with other owners. It is also a great opportunity to assess your own hound amongst others of quality. If you have a little knowledge of pedigrees it is fascinating to see the results of merging various bloodlines and watch the development of youngsters and their progress through the classes. As you talk with people you will hear many differing opinions, but it is wise not to allow yourself to be persuaded one way or another on the spur of the moment. It is better to store up all the information you glean and form your own ideas from the wide range of thoughts and theories you discuss or read about. Beware the person who unceasingly displays 'knowledge' about all matters Wolfhound, particularly in decrying exhibits other than his or her own. People who really understand the breed are seldom forthcoming with thoughts and information in public.

Ch Owenmore Cinniuint.

You can usually reason why one hound is placed higher than another by paying close attention to the judging on the day and always having the breed standard foremost in your mind. However, it is important to keep an open mind and never to assume that a hound is a poor specimen simply because it is not favoured, or that the first placed is necessarily the best or a near-perfect example of the breed. We all see hounds slightly differently, and the judge has the privilege of applying his or her interpretation of the breed standard and its ideals. Bear in mind that judging is subjective and one person's opinion on one day. The very same class of Wolfhounds would possibly be placed differently by another judge another (or even the same) day. Occasionally, opinions differ so widely that it is difficult to believe judges are working to the same criteria – for example, when a Best of

GB Ch Ballalyn's Himself. Photo: David Dalton

Breed (BOB) winner at one show is completely overlooked and unplaced in its class at the next. Confusing, to say the least, for those anxious to learn what constitutes a top-class Irish Wolfhound!

Apart from the vagaries of the judging, the 'other days' factor can play quite a large part in dog showing. Much depends on various factors, including the following:

- the moods of handler and hound.
- weather conditions, which affect some hounds more than others.
- length of journey to the show.

- Wolfhounds, like people, can have inexplicable days when they feel terrific and exude presence and personality or days when they are 'one degree under' and show accordingly.
- Some Wolfhounds take a dislike to a particular venue or show for no apparent reason. My own Ir Ch Owenmore Kingfisher enjoyed showing and invariably gave of his best throughout his career, but could never be persuaded to go well or do himself justice at that most important of events: the Breed Club Championship Show.

Whatever your placing, you are going home with the same beloved friend and companion with whom you arrived so full of hope, so never let disappointment be transferred. Rather, smile in defeat, congratulate the winners and learn to be philosophical about the judging. You may be surprised how many spectators notice generous and courteous behaviour, and it will gain you many friends. Do not be put off by the cynics who tell you you only have friends whilst you are losing.

Ch Owenmore Kittiwake, owned by A Killykeen-Doyle.

If you intend to breed, showing becomes almost essential. It presents the opportunity to have your hound assessed by knowledgeable breeders and a variety of judges, both breed specialists and all-rounders (those who judge many different breeds). Whilst it is always interesting to be judged by a specialist, many such judges have never judged another breed and consequently may fault judge or be overly biased towards specific breed points, tending to prefer a particular type. The experienced all-rounder probably has a more open mind, favouring the typical, well-balanced, free-moving hound, without giving undue weight to minor cosmetic points or over-exaggerations. During the course of a few seasons' showing you will have the opinion of a number of judges and, if your hound has been placed frequently, you are justified in believing it to be worthy breeding stock. Should you have the misfortune always to be overlooked it may be wise to revise your breeding plans.

Types of show

Rules and classification for shows differ between countries, but the basic showing format is the same. There are usually many different types of show. In Ireland we have Members, Limited and Open as well as Championship, while in Great Britain the shows are called Exemption, Primary, Limited, Sanction, Open and Championship. However, in all countries points towards the title *Champion* can only be gained at Championship shows. A list of shows for the forthcoming year is available from the national kennel club of each country and show secretaries advertise in national canine journals. Entries invariably close well in advance of the show date so it is essential to write early to be included on mailing lists. You can find out for which classes your hound is eligible by reading the schedule carefully. It is best to confine a puppy to classes for those of similar age (as a pup is always outclassed by older hounds) and to enter a previously-unshown mature hound in a class below Open to see how it rates. If it is placed first it will be eligible to compete against the Open class winner for Best Dog (or Bitch). Championship shows in all countries share the same principle: all unbeaten dogs and bitches go forward to compete for Best Dog or Bitch, then the two compete for Best of Breed (BOB). Only BOB winners compete in the Group class, and Group winners go forward for Best in Show (BIS).

The number of points or wins required to make up a Champion differs between Kennel Clubs, but Ireland remains the most difficult country in which to gain this coveted title as points awarded are dependent on the number of hounds actually exhibited at each show, and untitled dogs have to compete in the same class as Champions. In Great Britain you have to win three Challenge Certificates (CCs) under three different Championship judges

Learning how to show

If you are totally new to dog showing it is a good idea to attend a few shows as a spectator to get to know what will be expected of you in the ring. I wish I had been given such advice when I decided to show my first Wolfhound. Greatly experienced at showing horses under saddle, in-hand and even driven, I had never been to a dog show of any sort before entering a Championship show with my young bitch. I arrived just in time to see the final line-up of the previous class, so I found myself in the ring without a clue what to do. To my great good fortune the late Mrs Catherine Sutton (of Beagle fame) was judging. She showed me how to stand my pride and joy correctly, explaining what she was looking for and how she wanted the bitch moved. I am eternally grateful to that gracious lady and was pleased to have the opportunity, as I got to know her, of being able to joke about the incident. To this day I remind myself of her advice when exhibiting my hounds and try to emulate her thoughtfulness when judging. Newcomers must not expect this consideration, however; the onus is on the exhibitor to know what is required.

BIS: Aus Ch Clanmagael Amber (left); Reserve BIS: Aus Ch Baskerville Doolan.

As you watch from ringside, you will see that your hound must learn

- to trot proudly along beside you, on your left and in an anti-clockwise direction, taking no notice of those in front and behind
- to stand still, posed to its best advantage
- to allow the judge to inspect its teeth and to feel it all over whilst assessing conformation, possibly picking up its feet or taking its tail up between its hind legs towards the loin to ensure that length is sufficient (a tail of correct length will reach the spine)

NZ Ch Banrac Lady Crede at eight years.

When you are asked to move individually it will probably be in a triangle, always keeping the hound between yourself and the judge, so that movement can be assessed from all aspects. A further run away and back in a straight line may also be required before you are sent back into line to await placing.

Having noted all this and decided that showing is for you, you will be anxious to start working with your prospective champion. Show training classes (ringcraft classes) are held in many areas and it is a good idea to attend these to get your hound accustomed to standing still, being examined by strangers, and behaving sensibly among other dogs. At home try to get an experienced exhibitor to act as judge, watching you move your hound at different speeds. Some move better at a slower or faster rate than others, and an uncomfortable speed can unbalance a hound and ruin movement. Although the classic hound stance is head up, front legs parallel, well under to show off forechest, and with the hind leg nearest the judge slightly back from that nearest the handler, an experienced Wolfhound exhibitor will advise you on minor adjustments to this pose to accentuate better points or disguise less good ones.

NZ Ch Cinderscreek Tully at eight years.

If your hound is at all timid, take it out and about among people, traffic, shops, even football matches or parades – anywhere it can become accustomed to loud and sudden noises and clapping. A dog show is a very noisy place, so the more familiar your dog is with the general hubbub of life, the more relaxed and happy it will be there. Once you are familiar with show procedures and confident in your hound's ability to cope with the atmosphere, both of you will be ready to enter the ring with confidence and enjoy the occasion. Even the most experienced handlers feel a little nervous excitement at a big show, but remember that your feelings travel down the lead and affect performance, so it is worth working on your own temperament as well as that of your hound.

Preparation for the show

Showing is most enjoyable if you are well prepared and follow a routine. Grooming has been covered elsewhere but the most important point here is, if you feel your hound would benefit from a bath before a show, to do it several days beforehand. This allows the coat time to settle and some of the natural oils to return so that you can complete any final tidying. Do also remember to check that nails are short and ears and teeth are clean.

Ch Owenmore Ciara and family getting ready to be judged for the Brood Bitch and Progeny Class. Irish Wolfhound Club Championship Show 1995.

On the morning of a show it is best not to give your hound a large meal. If you give it anything beforehand, make it something light but nutritious, such as a can of sardines or two hard-boiled eggs. A hound seldom performs well on a full stomach and, while many do not care to relieve themselves in strange surroundings, it is a great embarrassment to you both if they choose to do so in the ring! Take a light meal to give your hound after the showing, and always be sure to take water from home; a change might upset the stomach, and fresh water is notoriously difficult to find at shows. I always take an electrolyte replacer with glucose to put into the water. It gives the hounds a boost and is especially beneficial in hot weather.

It is also a good idea to keep a show bag, packed with essentials and emergency supplies.These include:

- the show collar and lead
- grooming tools
- a small first aid kit

- a towel to dry the hound if wet, or to soak with water, wring out and drape over to cool him in the heat (an umbrella will serve the same purpose)
- food and water bowls
- titbits for bribery and reward
- electrolyte replacer
- most important – a poop-scoop and plastic bags to clean up if necessary

A spare ring number holder, hand wipes and a small emergency sewing kit complete my own show bag. I once split my trousers early on at a show and my poor husband spent ages trying to track down a needle and cotton so that I could effect repairs and hide my embarrassment!

The well-dressed handler and hound

One very important but frequently-overlooked aspect of the picture presented by you and your hound in the show ring is that of your own attire. Needless to say, comfortable shoes in which you can run are vital, as is tidy, unflamboyant dress, but it is also worth giving a little thought to colours worn: these can either set off and compliment or hide the hound. For instance, if your exhibit is dark grey and you stand behind it wearing black or any other dark colour, the judge cannot easily see a clear outline of the hound across the ring and may be attracted by one that is more visible. The whole point of showing is for your hound to catch and keep the judge's attention, so it is worth considering colour. Style, too, can be important. Voluminous flapping skirts take the eye from a Wolfhound on the move by creating a glamorous and fussy image, whereas an A-line skirt at knee length is practical and smart, as are trousers (preferably not jeans). At all times a handler should be as inconspicuous as possible, neither over- nor under-dressed – just discreetly complementary to his or her exhibit.

The collar and lead used are also worthy of some thought. If these can become invisible, so much the better. A thick or heavy collar shortens the neck and breaks up the hairline, and a thick lead or rope is awkward to manage. A fine chain and bootlace leather lead or the narrow cotton or nylon choker combination in a colour to blend with your hound looks good. Once you are out of the ring it is wise to use a stronger restraint.

In the ring

Once in the ring, keep an eye on the judge and listen to what he or she asks you to do. During a large class let your hound relax whilst others are being assessed. When the class is asked to move simultaneously, do not set off at the same instant as the person before you. Allow them to get ahead by a few strides, so that you can move your hound at its own best pace with space for the judge to get a clear view. Never let nerves panic you into hasty action. You are there (at great expense) to show your hound to very best advantage and to make the most of available ring space when asked to move alone. Plan exactly where to make the turns of your triangle and, should your hound set off at the wrong pace, take it back to the starting point and begin again, where possible with an apology to the judge.

Having returned to the line after your individual assessment, make much of your hound, possibly rewarding it with a favourite titbit. This makes the whole experience fun and enjoyable and paves the way for a happy and cooperative show career.

When standing your hound, do not fuss and constantly alter its leg positions; practice at home perfects the art of discreet adjustments through lead guidance or a change in your own position. Good judges prefer to see hounds stand naturally, and a well-made, balanced hound should not need posing. A good handler appears to do nothing and becomes invisible. Fussing draws the judge's attention and makes him wonder what you are trying to disguise. It has become fashionable in some quarters to kneel down beside a posed hound and hold its head up. This detracts from the innate dignity of the Wolfhound, even if it does give an illusion of height to one lacking in size. It is better to stand either in front, encouraging your dog to stretch its neck and look up at you, or well back from but level with its head, if necessary with a reassuring finger tickling cheek or jawbone to keep the head raised.

On the move a Wolfhound generally goes best on a loose lead, the ability to stretch the neck out slightly and carry the head at a natural angle allowing for greater forward reaching of the shoulder and overall freedom of movement. A hound and handler in harmony on the move is a pleasing sight, but

Hound and handler in harmony on the move. A nine-month-old puppy in free forward action.

The same puppy moving well towards the judge.

GB Ch Eaglescrag Kapitan.

many hounds have their potential for strong, free forward motion suppressed by the poor movement of their handlers. If the handler scuttles along with short, busy strides the hound does the same, whereas a longer, slower stride by the handler encourages reach and relaxation in the hound and gives the impression of going somewhere with purpose. It is surprising just how much influence handler stride length and pattern exerts, so it is well worth experimenting.

Free forward movement is sometimes taken to extremes by handlers, who race their hounds around the ring, presumably in an effort to disguise bad movement; since the judge sees only a blur of legs, it is impossible to tell whether they are being put down and picked up correctly. These people belong in the Afghan ring, where exuberance and flamboyance in movement are expected. In a Wolfhound, it is the ability to cover a great deal of ground at each stride with the minimum expenditure of energy which should be demonstrated – not speed.

Whilst practising with a loose lead it is beneficial to promote a good head carriage by carrying your hand fairly high, as hounds invariably look to the hand for guidance and praise. Those who deem a very high head carriage important often string their hound up so tightly that front feet barely touch the ground and the entire front assembly is given a totally straight and very unnatural appearance. Although this style of showmanship is prevalent in some countries, in Ireland the native breed is shown as naturally as possible.

GB Ch Drakesleat Odyt winning Reserve BIS at Crufts 1993.
Photo: Hartley

It is important, of course, that a hound is well-behaved and obedient in the ring, but I believe it is detrimental to have a Wolfhound trained to show like an automaton, afraid to relax and act naturally, as it removes all sighthound character and dignity. It is a poor judge who can only assess a hound of rigid demeanour and perfect stance.

If you never let the will to win at all costs become your driving force and can retain a sense of fun and humour, showing is a most enjoyable and educational experience. However long it takes, never give up hope of gaining a champion title or an elusive Group or BIS win. The pride, satisfaction and sheer joy when these goals are reached are indescribable and make all the frustration and effort worthwhile.

CHAPTER TEN

Mick following the lure.

LURE COURSING

Coursing has been a sport since man and hound first became friends and allies. Used primarily as a means of getting food or seeing off predators in ancient times, more recently it has become a competitive pastime and an exciting spectacle, as fit, healthy sighthounds rejoice in the function for which they were bred.

For those who prefer to watch Irish Wolfhounds behaving naturally and succumbing to inborn instinct rather than in the somewhat contrived and artificial world of the show ring, I can strongly recommend lure coursing. This organised sport has been carefully thought out and highly developed in the USA and Canada in particular, but is also enjoyed to a lesser degree in some other countries.

Lure coursing in the United States of America and Canada

I am fortunate in having as a friend John R Davies from New York State, an experienced competitor whose abiding interest is coursing and whose Wolfhounds are not only top winning coursers and American and Canadian field champions, but show and obedience champions as well. The triple titles are surely proof positive that beauty and functionality can and (in my opinion) should go hand-in-hand. To him I am indebted for information and can give no better or more enthusiastic introduction to this sport than to reproduce part of his letter to me. He writes:

Let me start by telling you why I think lure coursing is important. It is my opinion that most dog breeds have lost the skills for which they were first bred. Irish Wolfhounds are no exception. Dog owners talk and tell historic stories about what dogs of the past have done... all the great hunts! Those were the good old days when a dog could do the day's work that he had been bred to do. But that was the past and those days are gone, right?

It doesn't have to be.

All the qualities that were inherent in the dogs of the past are still contained in the genetic composition of today's hounds, although I must admit it is an ever growing diluted portion of the genetic composition. Most breeders today are only interested in selling puppies. Competing in the show ring and earning Champion titles gives them better credentials to sell puppies. I am not suggesting that the show ring is bad – it is extremely important! What I am saying is that the show ring only looks at one part of the dog, his looks (conformation to Standard). What about all the other parts that make a dog great, like brains, temperament and hunting skills? It is easy for me to see that if all the focus is on looks and nobody cares about anything else, pretty soon we will have good looking dogs that can't do anything. What good is a hunting dog that looks good but can't hunt?

The sport of lure coursing was developed in California in the 1970s specifically to test the hunting skills of sighthounds. As sighthounds, Irish Wolfhounds have (or should have) an instinctive desire to hunt by sight. This means they chase their prey until they catch and dispatch it. The lure in lure coursing represents the prey. Put simply, the hounds chase the lure (prey) and are evaluated on their performance. The areas being judged are ***enthusiasm, follow, speed, agility*** *and* ***endurance****. If you stop and think about a real hunt, you can see the importance of these qualities.*

Sir Michal Prince of Manor, JC, CD, FCh, Can FCh (otherwise known as 'Mick') demonstrates *enthusiasm*.

If a hound is not ***enthusiastic*** *about the hunt he will not perform well. His mind is on other things besides hunting. Perhaps he would rather be playing or maybe sleeping?*

Follow *is important, for if the hound gets unsighted during the hunt, the quarry will surely escape. No dinner tonight!*

Let's face it, the animals being hunted are fast. If the hound lacks the ***speed*** *and ease of movement to catch the prey and make the kill, I'm afraid we will have another hungry night.*

Agility *blends well with speed. Animals being chased don't run in a straight line. The hound must be able to adjust to sudden, unexpected turns.*

Lastly is ***endurance****. The hound must have enough stamina to last the hunt. In other words, they must be in good condition and possess the drive to get them to the finish line (the kill).*

I will be the first to admit that chasing a white plastic bag is different than chasing the real thing. On the other hand, I feel there are enough similarities to make this sport worthwhile, for it does in fact test the hound for the above characteristics. I am convinced that the hounds that do well in lure coursing would be the exceptional real game hunters. They possess that special something I call a keen natural instinct to hunt.

There are two organisations in the United States and one in Canada that sponsor lure coursing, but no matter which organisation is sponsoring the event, most things are the same. For example, there are always the same three coloured blankets – yellow, pink and blue. The hounds must wear colours so the judges can tell which is which as they run the course.

Next, hounds always run in groups of three, unless of course there are less hounds or some number like four where it would make more sense to run two groups of two.

The course layouts are of the same structure and things like sharp turns and long

Speed, as demonstrated by Am Ch Manor's Scarlet, FCh.
The two pictures show the action of a sighthound in full pursuit.

straight runs need to be incorporated into the course plan. Of course these must all fit the actual terrain of the land. Most courses are about 800 yards.

The equipment consists primarily of a direct current motor, which is usually an old automobile starter motor, mounted to a stand. A pulley is attached to the motor arm. There is a solenoid switch attached to the motor which is attached to a 12 volt battery. A control button on a long cord is wired into the unit which moves the motor each time the button is depressed. The battery which powers the equipment is hooked up to a battery charger so the charge doesn't run down as the equipment is being used. The motor stand assembly is

A champion stops for nothing –
even in the snow, Mick enjoys the activity for which he was bred.

nailed into the ground so it doesn't move around when the equipment is activated. Other equipment consists of pulleys, string and lures. There are two types of pulley – corner pulleys are used when the course changes direction and then there are hold down/up pulleys used in situations when the terrain has a dip or bump. There cannot be a large gap between the line and the ground so if the line is more than 4in off the ground a hold down pulley will be put in. In some instances it is necessary to hold the line up – the top of a hill is an example.

Int Ch Capitan of Shantamon winning a Hound Group.
Judge: A Killykeen-Doyle

The line is strong woven nylon string and forms a continuous loop. Starting from the motor pulley it is wound out around the course, pulley by pulley and finally back to the motor pulley where it is connected to form one loop. When the loop is attached to the motor pulley it moves every time the button is pressed.

The lures are white plastic garbage bags, unless of course it is snowing. In that instance, brown garbage bags are used. The bags are attached to the line. Usually there are three bags attached at 2m distance from each other.

You are now ready to course.

One thing I didn't mention about coursing is, it's a lot of fun! The hounds love it and look forward to going. The events are always held in scenic settings. It's kind of like being at a picnic. The mixture of sighthounds adds to the fun. I truly enjoy being with and sharing the day with all the sighthounds. Each has their own style of hunting and it's entertaining to watch them.

John R Davies
New York State

Another winner from the Nutstown kennel. A show champion is bred to be capable of sighthound pursuits.

Lure coursing field trials in the United States of America and Canada are run by sanctioned clubs with approved officials who organise and oversee all aspects of lure coursing. These include Chairman, Secretary, Clerk, Inspector (who checks that entered hounds are not lame but fit to run and that no bitches are in season), Lure Operator, Hunt Master and Judges. Only pure-bred, registered sighthounds are eligible to compete at these events and, before entering an official trial, they must prove their coursing ability by running a course with another hound of similar running style under the eye of a licensed judge, who will sign a pre-qualification certificate that must accompany the entry form the first time a hound is entered.

Sighthounds run and course just for the fun of it, but most owners and serious competitors like to work the hounds towards the titles that are on offer both from the American Sighthound Field Association (ASFA), the American Kennel Club (AKC) or the Canadian Sighthound Field Association (CSFA). Titles are earned on points gained according to placement under ASFA and CSFA rules, but a slightly different system is used by the AKC who is the newcomer organisation in lure coursing, becoming involved only about three years ago.

Despite their innate instincts, not all Wolfhounds chase the artificial lure without encouragement and training so, if you have a hound and would like to get involved in coursing, you should try to imprint chasing a lure as early as possible by playing chase and fetch games, particularly with a puppy or youngster. It goes without saying that hounds must be in good condition and worked carefully to a state of physical fitness, and that puppies and young hounds must be brought on slowly and not over-exercised. If you are trying an adult hound, do not be dismayed if it won't run or chase at the first attempt; try several times, preferably with different hounds as partners, and it might suddenly decide coursing is great fun.

Lure coursing in Great Britain

There is quite a flourishing coursing club in England run by Wolfhound enthusiasts, but it is not as structured or competitive as those in North America and Germany. Here the emphasis is more on fun and the friendly gathering of like-minded people who enjoy encouraging their hounds' hunting abilities. Organisation depends on who turns up on the day, but the actual courses are very seriously contested with points awarded towards trophies and prizes at the end of the season. Each meeting is a great social outing, and a wonderfully relaxed way of getting to know people and seeing hounds really enjoying themselves.

Lure coursing in Ireland

Although there is no official Wolfhound coursing club here, a few enthusiasts gather occasionally to run their hounds and once a year, at the Irish Breeds Group Championship Show, an organised lure coursing competition is held and prizes are awarded by a generous sponsor.

Lure coursing in Germany

Although lure coursing has been practised in Germany for some time, it was only in 1995 that the Race Commission drafted a formal set of rules and regulations to govern it, and these rules were formally voted upon and accepted at the Annual Meeting in March 1996.

All sighthounds with Fédération Cynologique Internationale (FCI) pedigrees and German Sighthound Club (DWZRV) registered sighthounds with a coursing licence may take part. To earn a coursing licence a dog must run clean six times with one other dog, preferably of the same running style. This means they must course twice on each of three different occasions. The dog being tested must wear a muzzle and coursing blanket.

Aus Ch Planhaven Morgan and Aus Ch Marumac Alfred top the NSW Championship Show, 1993.
Irish Wolfhounds all over the world are bred to be active as well as beautiful.

The Trial Officials, equipment used and course layout are very similar to those of the ASFA, but the hounds run in pairs wearing red or white coursing blankets and are muzzled. Points are awarded towards the three possible titles, but to gain a coursing title a hound must also have rated Excellent from the adult classes at a DWZRV Championship Show. Apart from gaining its German titles, a hound may also become an FCI International Coursing Champion. As in the USA and Canada, the events are extremely well run in beautiful countryside by very knowledgeable people, the prime concern being the welfare and enjoyment of the hounds.

In conclusion...

Lure coursing is undoubtedly a spectacle well worth going along to watch or take part in. By doing so you can learn more about, and truly appreciate, the beauty and awesome speed, agility and grace of Irish Wolfhounds in full flight succumbing to their natural instinct for the chase.

I will leave readers with the controversial thought that there is a case to be made for show hounds having to demonstrate their speed, stamina and chasing abilities before being awarded a full champion title. This would help to enforce Captain Graham's dictum and ensure that unsound hounds do not gain this accolade.

CHAPTER ELEVEN

Four Superstar males in *Down/stay.*

OBEDIENCE

The Irish Wolfhound is not a breed that springs instantly to mind when mention is made of obedience, let alone obedience trials. Most Wolfhound owners of my acquaintance are slightly surprised or, in some cases, positively amazed when their hound deigns to come back or pay any heed at all when called. The thought of aspiring to *Sit* or *Heel* on command is almost beyond comprehension, these being words many of us tentatively use more in hope than expectation. I do not mean to imply that this is an acceptable state of affairs: indeed, with such large creatures in our care, it is positively irresponsible not to train them in the basics at the very least. This especially applies to the urban dweller whose hound may be at large in public places, but there is really no good excuse for country dwellers or land owners not to instil some discipline to exercise control.

Being one of the many *hoping* for some display of obedience from my hounds rather than *working positively* towards it, I am unable, in all conscience, to write or advise on the subject, so I decided to go right to the top for help for this chapter. I am indebted to Connie Banks of the Superstar Wolfhounds, Canada. Not only does she very successfully show her beautiful hounds, making up many champions, but she also has the distinction of producing excellent results in the obedience ring. In 1993 her Dual Ch Superstar In Neon became the first Irish Wolfhound ever to gain the coveted Obedience Trial Champion title – the very highest level in obedience training. The prefix 'Dual Ch' indicates that the hound has become a show and obedience champion.

Connie shows a deep love and understanding of the Wolfhound psyche and a real desire and need to be as one with her hounds. All owners of this breed will, I am sure, benefit from reading carefully what she has to say and taking heed. It may even inspire those who, although they do not enjoy showing and have no opportunity to take their hounds coursing, would nevertheless like to participate in something with their beloved companion. I am very grateful to her for the following contribution.

WOLFHOUNDS IN OBEDIENCE

Have you ever witnessed a Wolfhound not only clear a 90cm (3ft) bar jump but follow a distant hand signal direction indicating which structure to leap? Have you held your breath in suspense while the massive beast extends his mighty neck to scent carefully, select and retrieve his owner's personally handled article amongst a set of placebos? Have you seen a Wolfhound respond diligently to the beckon only to be interrupted in motion by a non-verbal command to drop, freeze and await further instruction? If you answered yes, you can attest to the potential of an Irish Wolfhound in the Obedience ring. The examples given are some of the most advanced exercises. It is not necessary to train your dog to this degree. However, it is possible. In 1993 my Dual Champion and Obedience Trial Champion Superstar in Neon became the first Irish Wolfhound to garner the OT.CH prefix. Dual indicates he is both a conformation (show) champion and an obedience trial champion. The successful completion of the exercises described are just some of the requirements of the obedience trial champion.

For every Wolfhound that works in obedience there will be critics of the sport or, more specifically, the Wolfhounds' involvement. Some people seriously believe a Wolfhound is not suitable for obedience training. Bunk! The training relationship is everything a Wolfhound desires, which includes time together, patience, mutual respect, trust and affection. Without these elements training cannot be fostered. It is impossible to force a Wolfhound to work. Proper use of guidance and reinforcement will help a Wolfhound to develop an understanding that it is in its best interest to respond in a favourable manner. There is nothing negative about this concept. If your Wolfhound is willing to work for you, it obviously thinks it is worth doing. In other words, there is something in it for the hound too. Basic obedience training is a reward in itself. Advanced training is, of course, more challenging, but very gratifying to both the Wolfhound and the owner. Many factors modify the degree of success and the amount of time to reach it, but every trainer should start with a positive, optimistic and realistic attitude.

You chose an Irish Wolfhound for all the right reasons. The dignity, courage, intelligence, affection and loyalty have attracted you to the breed. You appreciate their size, presence and power, yet their gentleness is the first trait you notice. Although they often display an aloofness with strangers, the intense devotion to their own people is always most evident. They possess an innate desire for a close relationship with the people in their life. The rôle of guardian, but never guard dog, is a popular avocation for many Irish Wolfhounds. They have no difficulty demonstrating a desire to please. Irish Wolfhounds thrive in a stimulating environment provided by their people. Seeing a Wolfhound in these terms, it is rather disappointing more owners do not consider obedience training for their hounds.

Obedience training offers so much to both the dog and the owner. Do not be misled with fallacies about disgracing dignity, breaking spirit, Wolfhounds being 'above' tricks, or anything that undermines the concept of positive training. Anyone using those excuses has never experienced the joy and rewards of a trained, well-mannered Irish Wolfhound. Negative training methods that emphasise punishment, oppression and pain have long vanished with the overwhelming success of motivational teaching. These more pleasant techniques work well with all breeds and trainers willing to implement them. It is not necessary to be a highly-skilled, fully-knowledgeable, experienced professional trainer to teach your Irish Wolfhound the basics. Every owner with the time, patience and interest can achieve the requirements of an obedience trained dog, whether competition is a consideration or not. The close attachment between a Wolfhound and its human family is often the characteristic that draws us to the breed. The process of training provides the greatest opportunity to develop and strengthen this bond. Through training, communication, reward and fulfilment are exchanged. As training proceeds, understanding and appreciation for each other are also enhanced. Courage, dignity, intelligence and gentleness, which are desirable breed traits, all flourish with a supportive training relationship.

Preparation

If your full-grown Wolfhound has still not begun training, do not despair. It is never too late. Many adult Wolfhounds are not obedience trained until they finish competing in the conformation (show) ring or coursing field. Others have made such wonderful, well-behaved pets their owners didn't feel training was required until they grew huge. Adult hounds can be trained quite successfully. However, if at all possible, your puppy should begin training early in life. Preparation in the form of early puppyhood education can make things so much easier.

Socialisation is another term for pre-training. It is impossible to over-emphasise the need and importance of socialisation of every Wolfhound puppy, but especially one expected to undergo training later in life. As in most physical and mental activities, there is stress involved in training. Puppies can be conditioned to deal effectively with stress through early handling. All responsible, caring breeders understand this concept and apply the principle. They take care to touch, hold and stroke puppies from birth. This practice should be limited strictly to the owners of the dam; under no circumstances should strangers be permitted to disturb nursing pups or their mother.

The pups begin to show interest in their surroundings at three weeks old; by four weeks they are interacting with their litter-mates; by five weeks they love everything and fear nothing. Human contact is important at all stages and socialisation should not be limited to their canine families. Early human intervention and bonding has a positive effect on the future personality and long-term trainability of the pup.

Wolfhounds are born with an innate compatibility for other dogs. This social characteristic needs no special fostering. Many Wolfhound breeders keep their hounds in a pack environment, which would often be unheard of in some of the non-hound breeds. Their sociable affection for each other comes naturally to them, but it is important to work at human bonding to encourage independence from the pack mentality.

Puppies soon learn the people in their life provide them with the necessities their mother once offered, such as food, cleaning, comfort and affection. They learn about the safe, secure environment we offer. They learn that life can be enjoyable in your presence. Dogs learn when they realise they benefit as a result of what they do. Their actions can produce a reward or satisfying experience. Although your Wolfhound enjoys your company and affection, it will still require your assistance in making the most of training. Be fair, honest and kind. Your puppy will learn to respond favourably to you. Loving you, it enjoys receiving rewards from you such as praise, touching and treats. These can be used as motivation and reinforcement in training. There is always a great advantage in training a dog that loves, trusts and respect you. These emotions are not difficult to find in your Irish Wolfhound.

Obedience prospect

After a few visits to the obedience trials you will notice Wolfhounds are not the most popular entries. Few people purchase a Wolfhound to excel in the all-breed obedience competition. If you are looking for nothing other than a top scoring dog, do not consider this wonderful breed. Leave the Irish Wolfhounds for those who appreciate more than their ability for high performance. However, if you love the breed for what it is and wish to make the best of your hound through training, here are a few tips for selecting a good candidate.

When you are choosing a puppy, the most valuable advice comes from the breeder who knows the puppies and has been familiar with them since day one. Ask the breeder to describe any differences he or she has noticed in the development of the pups. Inquire about the activity level of the pups rather than judging the behaviour for yourself on any given day. You might be interested to know which pups are dominant, sensitive to noise, greedy at the feed dish or anything else, so don't be afraid to ask. Tell the breeder you are considering future obedience work and he or she should be able to assist you in selecting a potential puppy.

I look for puppies that are outgoing, active, attentive, confident, friendly, playful and happy. As an obedience candidate I prefer a dominant pup rather than a submissive one. Remember, we are talking about Irish Wolfhound puppies, not a breed with a tendency towards aggression. Do not confuse dominance with aggression. I do not believe unexplained aggression toward people is possible in a Wolfhound. If a Wolfhound is vicious it has been made that way, not born that way. Shyness in the breed is more common than aggression. A shy Wolfhound has trouble adapting to new and different surroundings. It will take much patience for it to become a competitive obedience prospect. However, if your Wolfhound is shy, I strongly recommend obedience training, not for competition, but as a confidence-building exercise. Start socialisation as soon as you get your new puppy to prevent future shyness.

Some pups show more interest in watching and following you. This is a positive trait and I am always looking for those pups. Although this behaviour seems to come more naturally to some, it can also be developed in a puppy by training. As sighthounds, Irish Wolfhounds by instinct are interested in movement. As an obedience prospect, you want your hound to be interested in watching and paying attention to you. Eye contact is a significant feature in training and canine behaviour. In this context, eye contact is not related to the dominant behaviour in staring down another. Long before formal training starts, encourage and lavishly praise your pup for giving you eye contact. If your puppy is looking at you you have its attention. Attention is critical when you communicate during training or any other time.

Again, rely on the breeder's experience to evaluate the temperament of the parents. Since you have chosen an honest, reputable breeder, this person is your best source for describing the personality, intelligence and attentiveness of your pup's father and mother. Even if these dogs were not formally trained or do not hold obedience titles, the experienced breeder will know how they demonstrate these traits in normal daily activity. Socialisation is effective, but temperament is also determined by genetic factors. Many personality traits affecting training, such as attentiveness and willingness, are passed down genetically. Parents with a desire to please often produce this willingness and tractability in their offspring. Such pups are easier to obedience train than those who are aloof and independent.

The mother teaches the litter by the example she sets. A confident, calm, affectionate mother demonstrates security. The pups learn they have nothing to fear. This encourages them to explore on their own and accept new situations, which provide stimulation. Every time a puppy experiences a positive challenge, it becomes more eager to attempt others. The secure environment builds a foundation and contributes to the pup's potential.

Learning

Irish Wolfhounds are intelligent and every owner admires them for it. However, intelligence can be interpreted and proved by various means. Try to understand your dog, but do not attempt to define or put limits on its intelligence. Life experience and training develop this, so you as an owner have a responsibility to your dog. Although you should not limit or underestimate your dog's ability, make your training fair by setting attainable goals. Realistic expectations are necessary. Many dogs and their owners triumphantly exceed their original expectations, but this scenario is much more desirable than failing to meet unreasonable demands. Understanding your dog also helps you devise a personalised training technique that will work best and avoid methods that may be detrimental to progress.

Your Wolfhound, like all dogs, has inherited certain behaviours through genetics. Sporting dogs, working dogs, hounds and others are genetically predisposed to perform a task instinctively. The sighthound breeds, including the Irish Wolfhound, have a natural ability to hunt unassisted by man. They have a keen sense of sight, pursuit and speed. Wolfhounds have an inherent sense to detect motion. They are coursing hounds. This predisposition affects obedience training. Be aware of your Wolfhound's instinctive ability so that you can work with it realistically rather than against it. If its hunting instinct dominates its behaviour you must incorporate sight and action into your training strategy.

Aside from instinct, your Wolfhound exercises its ability through what it learns, and learns a range of behaviours through experience. Complex problems can be solved by an ingenious Wolfhound who has learnt how to benefit from the situation. If it opens doors, howls to go out, drinks from the fountain, or performs similar bright moves, it is demonstrating its skills. However, these skills have been taught, intentionally or otherwise. A dog soon learns a behaviour when it is reinforced. In other words, its actions are reinforced because they achieve a desired result. The more opportunity your dog has, the more it learns. Very often, these brilliant hounds make demands on their people. Consider this positive. These bright, persistent Wolfhounds are fun to train and are great obedience prospects.

All Wolfhounds can be trained, but I have found some easier to teach than others. Perhaps saying some approach training in a different style from others describes it more accurately. Trainability is a reflection of personality. Never confuse intelligence with trainability. Many incredibly intelligent dogs are most difficult to train. Wolfhounds vary in their intensity of desire to please or cooperate with their owner. This personality trait is both genetic and acquired through socialisation. Diversity exists between and within families in the breed. All other factors being equal, I have noticed certain families and/or individual hounds to be predisposed with a keen interest in and attentiveness to human interaction. Obviously I prefer this personality for obedience work.

Every puppy can be nurtured to develop its trainability. Early intervention and stimulation make a dramatic impact. A pup that has positive experience with a wide range of activities, sights, sounds and smells grows up into a well-adjusted hound. Such a pup dedicates its attention to its trainer, rather than trying hopelessly to overcome distractions in the environment. It will be calm and not easily frustrated if it has been exposed to a variety of situations early in life. Training a hound who is afraid of everything outside its own little world is difficult. Trainability can be strengthened in puppyhood by teaching that it is safe and rewarding to leave home in the company of its people. This is done by taking your puppy to as many places as possible and making it a positive experience. Go prepared with food, treats, water, extra time for rest and affection and you will both enjoy the excursion. Let children touch your pup and talk to it. Senior citizens should be invited to get close and stroke it. Don't scare your youngster, but don't go out of the way to avoid every single loud noise or unusual commotion. Help your dog to investigate anything that attracts its interest. Do not force it to do something it resists through lack of confidence, and do not reinforce shyness with sympathy. Just offer support through praise. Help the pup to build more faith in itself and it will soon overcome the obstacle. This all adds up to valuable practice for future training, where again you will encourage your young hound to conquer the challenge through your guidance. In short, you can help your pup develop an interest and desire to respond to your commands for use in training.

Tips

There are many excellent books and videos on obedience and canine behaviour. Study as many as possible to get a good grasp of positive motivational training. Participate in a class if you enjoy working with other people. Classes provide instruction, socialisation and a place to practise. Choose methods you understand and with which you feel comfortable. A complete training manual is beyond the scope of this book, but I have included some ideas which work for me while training my Wolfhounds in the basics.

Set realistic goals. Don't expect to have a Utility Wolfhound in six months by training 15 minutes a week! Start with the basics. Every Wolfhound can learn the idea of *Come, Sit, Down* and *Stay* in a few weeks. Once these have been mastered, you will have a better concept of the required commitment to carry on in obedience training. As you train you will notice how your hound's ability to learn new skills improves. Dogs learn to learn. The more you teach them, the easier the new task will be learned.

Dual Ch/OT Ch Superstar in Neon clearing a 90cm jump. Photo: Kevin Proud

Be aware of your dog's physical and mental soundness. Ideally your obedience hound should be totally sound. If not, you must compromise. An unsound dog is no exemption for training, but you must help it to compensate. Set your standards accordingly. Do not try to teach it something that causes discomfort. Do not try to train an unhealthy dog. Attend to its health requirements. Health is a priority.

Wolfhound puppies grow very big very fast. They are easily and often tired. Don't push your puppy. If it is too tired to play, it is too tired to work. Usually your puppy lets you know if it is tired by lack of enthusiasm to do anything. Back off with the training for a while and let your pup rest.

Never undermine your Irish Wolfhound. Give it credit for all it does. Forgive its mistakes. You should not think less of your young hound if it cannot do everything you want. If you do not feel you have the world's greatest dog, your dog has the wrong owner.

Before teaching anything else, train your dog to pay attention. This is outlined in the next section. Don't expect your dog to obey your command if it is not watching and listening to you attentively. Never give a command during training without first getting your dog's attention. Just as important, don't assume your dog must continue to focus on you after the training session is over. Teach the release command, which is also in the next section.

Make your training sessions short and sweet. Twice a day, 10 minutes each time, is plenty. Keep your dog interested and learn how to balance consistency and variety. Always end on a positive. If your dog is having a terrible day, let it succeed at one tiny task, praise, release and finish for the day. If it's a terrific day and your dog does something absolutely amazing in the first two minutes, finish and play with it. Wolfhounds love fun.

Don't be afraid to try new ideas. Good trainers are always open to change. Learn to be flexible and imaginative. Be patient but do not continually labour on something that is not working. Come up with a better, more effective plan.

Wolfhounds are attracted to action and react to body language. Make your motions emphatic. During heeling, set an example by moving around energetically. Be calm and smooth during *sits, downs* and *stays.*

Wolfhounds are stubborn. This is a positive. Being stubborn means your hound tries persistently to get what it wants. Since you can provide what it wants, you can very easily teach how to get it. Find out exactly what it wants more than anything else in the world and use that as your reinforcement.

Positive reinforcement does not need to be tangible. It can be another more desirable behaviour, such as going for a drive, coursing the field, swimming, playing or whatever other activity your hound really enjoys. Of course you must still praise your dog the moment it responds correctly to your command, but you can save its 'reward' activity for immediately after the session.

Never strike your dog during training. Discontinue training indefinitely if you feel a need to punish your dog physically for what you consider disobedience or lack of cooperation. This is not the sport for you. Dogs do not disobey out of revenge, spite, arrogance or a multitude of other sins humans ascribe to them. It is not in their nature to act that way. If your hound does not obey you, it is simply because you have not trained it correctly. Even if it is a command you have taught, if your hound does not respond appropriately, usually it is because you have not trained it thoroughly and it does not understand.

Teach your dog to do what is right, rather than not to do what is wrong. Reinforce correct behaviour while your dog exhibits it. Ignore incorrect behaviour.

Training does not necessarily mean competing in obedience trials or obtaining titles. Train for the personal satisfaction of developing a bond with your dog. Although I rarely enter competitions, I love to train and work with my hounds in everyday life. Train for enjoyment and understanding: scores are just a bonus.

Never underestimate the power of love. No, your Wolfhound will not obey you simply because you love each other, but the emotion certainly intensifies the communication. You cannot bluff a dog. It knows how you feel. Don't be ashamed to express your love for your dog openly during training or any other time. Your praise is much more meaningful. Your hound is your partner, so work as a team. Both members will feel good about sharing the joy, excitement and triumph. An honest training relationship is guaranteed to enhance the bond, but the love must be there to begin with.

I have spent 25 years living with many Irish Wolfhounds. They are the love of my life. It is difficult to pick one single most enjoyable activity in which we participate together. Sharing life and love with them is ecstasy, raising litters is a joy, titling champions is victorious, coursing is exhilarating, to name a few; but the bond that develops through the process of obedience teamwork makes the magic of training the best.

Four-month-old Superstar in Cyberspace giving Connie complete attention.

Lessons

Attention: This is fun to teach and very important. Attention requires having your dog's eye contact and alert readiness for whatever follows. Although attention can be trained formally, I rarely use a specific command word with a trained dog. In the early stages I might use the *Watch me* or just the dog's name. In time, I want the dog to pay attention with eye contact on any of the given commands, such as *Sit*, *Heel* or *Stay*.

Starting with a very young puppy, I first use food treats to get its interest. Hold the treat near your face then praise and reward your pup for looking up. The praise must be immediate, no later, if you want to reinforce the behaviour. It is then released with *Okay,* which is explained in the next section. Later, hold the treat at your side. When your pup looks at you instead of the treat, praise and give the treat. Next, hold the treat behind your back where it is not visible. Praise the pup at the precise moment it looks at you and then give the treat.

Whether you are training, playing or doing anything else, always take advantage of every opportunity to reinforce eye contact. Food treats are not necessary in every situation. Reinforcement is something different to every dog. It might be petting, verbal praise, a toy, a game or anything the dog enjoys.

Especially if you are training for competition, be certain to play eye contact games while your dog is sitting directly in front of you and while it is sitting or walking in the heel position beside you. Eye contact in motion can be taught by walking with your dog. Take a few steps with the dog beside you. Wait for it to look up at you. The moment it does, praise and release. Extend the eye contact duration by praising for the behaviour at the time, but wait longer to release.

I also practise attention with older dogs by incorporating it into the stand for examination exercise. This works best for dogs that are solid on the stay. The dog is placed in a stand and stay, then I take several steps away from it. Walking from side to side, but remaining in its field of vision, I constantly praise it for focussing its attention on me. When eye contact is very intense, I walk back and touch it. This is repeated a few times, then I release.

As training progresses, you will want the dog to maintain its attention throughout the other exercises. Always reinforce spontaneous eye contact and attention from your hound.

Release: Don't expect your Wolfhound to be in the working mode or staring into your eyes all the time. It is not natural. There are occasions when your dog needs only to be well behaved, not under strict control. It is perfectly acceptable to take your dog for a walk without keeping it in the heel position. Let your dog know when it can take it easy. I use the word *Okay* and motion with my hands to let my dog know when it can relax.

During training, always allow your dog to relax after the successful completion of any task. The release in itself is a reinforcement for positive behaviour if properly timed. The anticipation of the sheer enjoyment and excitement of the release contributes to dogs working happily. If you are using food during training it should be given before the release.

The release should be a big occasion when a dog is making progress in a troublesome area. It needs a stress reliever just as much as you do. There is no need to end the training session after you release the dog on a particular exercise; just allow a short break, and then go back to work again. Many exercises are trained in steps, so releases are necessary for individual steps, rather than waiting for the dog to learn the entire sequence of steps in the exercise. Although training sessions must always be brief, use the release many times throughout.

Sit: Although sitting is not a Wolfhound's most natural position, it is very easily taught, especially to a young puppy. While standing and facing the puppy, coax it with a food treat to come close to you. Hold the treat in your hand directly below your knees and allow your pup to take it when it gets close enough. Of course, there will be some variation in the position according to the size of the puppy, but this close proximity usually automatically encourages your pup to sit. In the early stages no command is necessary. You want your pup to know that in front of you is a wonderful place to sit. They never forget it.

If the puppy is older and more energetic, follow the same steps to get it in front of you, but use the *Sit* command as you raise the treat slightly above, back and over its eyebrows. It will have to sit to reach the treat. Let it take the treat as soon as its rump goes down. Practise a few times, then release. Always praise your hound when it sits near you and exhibits polite manners.

Sit is an important command. Instead of telling your hound what not to do, tell it to sit. Sitting is not compatible with most unacceptable behaviours. Tell your young Wolfhound to sit when it is impatient just before meals or walks. If you don't want your pup jumping up at you, tell it to sit.

Down: While the puppy is still small, I sit on the floor with it to teach the *Down*. The pup, in a sitting position, is shown a treat slightly below its nose. Lower the treat in your hand for it to follow into the *down* position, giving the *Down* command. Let your pup have the treat as soon as it touches the floor. Praise and release. Encourage your pup to stay down until you have actually released it. In time, emphasise with a hand signal rather than a food treat. I use the palm of my right hand as a down signal.

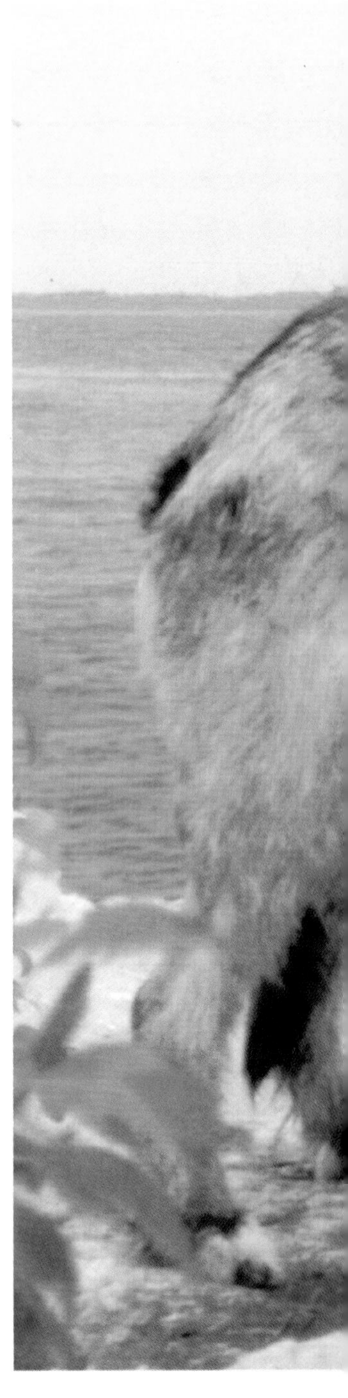

Dual Ch/OT Ch Superstar in Neon on Georgian Bay. Photo: Kevin Proud

Food works wonders while training is in progress, especially with young puppies, but your goal is to train for willingness and understanding. This applies to all exercises. It takes time, patience and positive reinforcement of the appropriate behaviour. There is nothing wrong with using edibles in training, but they should be considered an added bonus rather than the sole reason for compliance. You should not offer food for every move your dog makes. Keep it a secret when the treat is coming. Miss a few turns and then suddenly surprise your hound with a goody. This is not being unfair to your dog. It is a fun game, guaranteed to keep your hound's interest.

Recall: I often hear Wolfhound owners complain their dogs won't come when called. The sighthound instinct can easily be convinced there are better things to do than return to the owner! Understanding this will help you prepare for successful training of the recall. You must make the *Come* exercise fun, fast and immensely rewarding.

Start teaching your puppy the recall very informally. When it seems to be thinking of coming to you, call your pup exuberantly and make a big fuss of it when it reaches you. Be sitting on the ground and playfully grab your pup in your arms when it arrives.

With an older puppy or adult, try calling and then running in the opposite direction. Be prepared with a reward. For speedy recalls, you can show your hound its favourite toy, call it by name, but then throw the toy directly behind you when your hound reaches you part way. Give the release as it goes for the toy and meet your hound with it. Praise your hound verbally and touch it.

Wolfhounds love to watch movement and give chase. Take advantage of their natural ability. If you are with someone the dog knows well, ask the person to hold his collar and run a good distance from them. Call your hound as you run and ask your helper to set it free. Make a big fuss when it reaches you. Extend this 'tag' game to hide-and-seek by hiding in the tall grass or behind a tree. Let your hound find you and praise it for doing the job so well. There is no need to teach your hound to sit in front at this point. That is a separate exercise, necessary only if you choose to compete at trials.

Do not let your Wolfhound run freely in an area where there are risks to its safety. Never call your dog before you have its attention. Never call it when you cannot rely on the command. Instead, get closer to your dog, get eye contact and give the command when it is paying attention to you. Don't put an untrained dog in a situation geared to fail. Every event is a practice for the future.

Don't teach your dog to ignore your command by allowing it to do so. If it is overwhelmed by some other attraction, approach your dog calmly, gently place it on a lead, get its attention, cheerfully say its name and *Let's go* and walk away from the distraction. Do not jerk the lead. Praise your dog the entire time as you walk away to keep its attention. Never punish it for a poor recall. Failed commands are training inadequacies and must not be confused with defiance. Do not lose your temper or you will lose much more than that.

Stay: The *stay* is simple to teach but should be carefully done. When taught with too much correction, it can easily destroy all the confidence your hound has worked hard to establish. Confidence is required in learning all new skills. Lack of it slows the learning process because the dog is afraid to be wrong. This is an obstacle we must overcome, especially in the Irish Wolfhound with its soft, sensitive nature. A Wolfhound needs all the confidence-building possible. It must be reassured that it will not be punished for trying, no matter how incorrectly it performs.

Start your stays from the sitting position by telling your hound to *Stay,* but remain within reach. If it is unsteady hold its collar gently. After a few seconds, praise and release. Try it a bit further away. Let your dog hold the stay for just a few seconds, then praise and release. An older puppy can be placed in a stay while you walk away. Return to it, praise, walk away again, return again and praise again. This can be repeated several times as long as you reinforce the stay by praising your pup for remaining seated. In time, extend the distance and duration.

Your dog should be focussing its attention on you while it is on a stay. If its attention is elsewhere, you need to go back and practise attention exercises. If the dog breaks the stay command, quietly return it to where you left it and start again. Do not punish the dog for moving or it will become reluctant to do anything after being placed in a stay. In the learning stages, always return to the dog to release rather than releasing from a distance or giving another command.

Never combine the stay and recall until the hound is totally reliable in both areas. If I practise the two together, it is done while someone holds the pup's collar and releases it when I call, as explained in the recall. Make it a game and it is destined to succeed. I use the *stay* command infrequently, preferring to teach a dog to remain in position, namely *sit* or *down,* until it is given the release or further instruction.

Heel: Irish Wolfhounds enjoy going for walks with their people. Make the activity a pleasure by teaching your hound to walk with you attentively. Proper heeling takes time. It improves with practice. Start teaching your puppy while it is young but don't expect it to heel perfectly. Teach it to walk rather than heel. I always play walking games with my puppies. A lead is never used, but I stay indoors or in a safe area outside. It's fun to play because puppies follow naturally. Stand with the puppy at your left side, both facing the same direction. Hold a treat in your hand. Do not use the heel command but say *Let's go* in a happy voice. Get your pup's attention and, when it looks up, take a couple of quick, short steps. If your pup moves with you, give it the treat and release. Just do it for a few seconds at first, gradually extending and varying the distance.

With older pups, walk several steps, reinforcing eye contact with verbal praise, and then release and throw a toy or treat in the exact direction in which you have been walking. Break, then start again. Praise your pup for staying close to your left side and paying attention. Ignore your pup if it walks away from you. Do not expect your pup to twist its neck around and stare into your eyes at every step of the way. This would be uncomfortable and unnatural. However, it is reasonable to expect your dog to look up and check with you periodically.

Eventually you will need to walk your dog on a lead in a public place. Follow the same routine. Do not be tempted to jerk your dog on the lead as this will undo what it has learnt. Encourage your dog to focus on you rather than following the lead. If it pulls on the leash, stop and wait for it to notice that you are not moving. The moment your dog looks at you, praise and walk again. Repeat this as often as necessary. If your dog walks calmly but doesn't seem to be paying attention to you, wait until it looks at you. Then immediately praise and give it a treat.

When you start the actual heeling exercise use the same ideas. Heel means to be in position at your left side, whether moving or stopped. The command includes sitting at your left side when stopped. The sit must be automatic but, in the early stages, use the *sit* command when you stop. Praise the *sit*. Several short starts and stops, while reinforcing the *sit* with praise, soon teach your dog to sit automatically.

Be careful not to correct poor heeling. It is simply a lack of training and will improve with proper teaching and practice. Concentrate on reinforcing proper heeling and ignoring heeling that is out of position. Show your dog where it should be rather than correcting it for being where it shouldn't be. Be patient.

Retrieve: Start playing *fetch* with very young puppies. Soft cloth toys make an excellent first dumbbell. Sit on the floor or grass and let the pup pull on the toy as you hold it. Get the puppy excited and, as soon as it lets go of it, say *Take it* and throw it while the pup watches you. Most puppies are thrilled to chase it and bring it back for more fun. Whenever the pup retrieves, praise it, quickly grab the toy and continue the game. My puppies will repeat this several times. If the pup looks as if it has had enough and is starting to get bored, don't throw the toy again. Continue playing this fetch game as the pup grows.

Even if your dog is not so keen when it gets a bit older, it has learnt the idea of retrieving. Getting an adult Wolfhound to run for a thrown object is one thing; getting it to bring it back is another. I prefer to teach my hounds to hold and carry the dumbbell first. This, too, takes patience with a Wolfhound who has never had the experience of playing with and carrying hard objects before.

Training the forced retrieve with proper use of the ear pinch may be a consideration. Many excellent training books such as *Beyond Basic Dog Obedience* by Diane L Bauman provide complete instructions for the forced retrieve. In a nutshell, the ear pinch involves pinching the dog's ear just enough to teach it to open its mouth for the dumbbell. As soon as it opens and takes the dumbbell, the pinch is released, with loads of praise. It is a very temporary measure, not necessary once the dog learns what is required. I have found the dogs that played fetch games as pups catch on much faster and only require the pinch a few times.

Do not use the ear pinch if you are uncomfortable with the idea. It often hurts the pincher more than the *pinchee.* It is not suitable for everyone. Never use it if you cannot effectively follow through with it. No, Wolfhounds do not enjoy the pinch but, after implementing it briefly, I have witnessed them become confident, reliable retrievers.

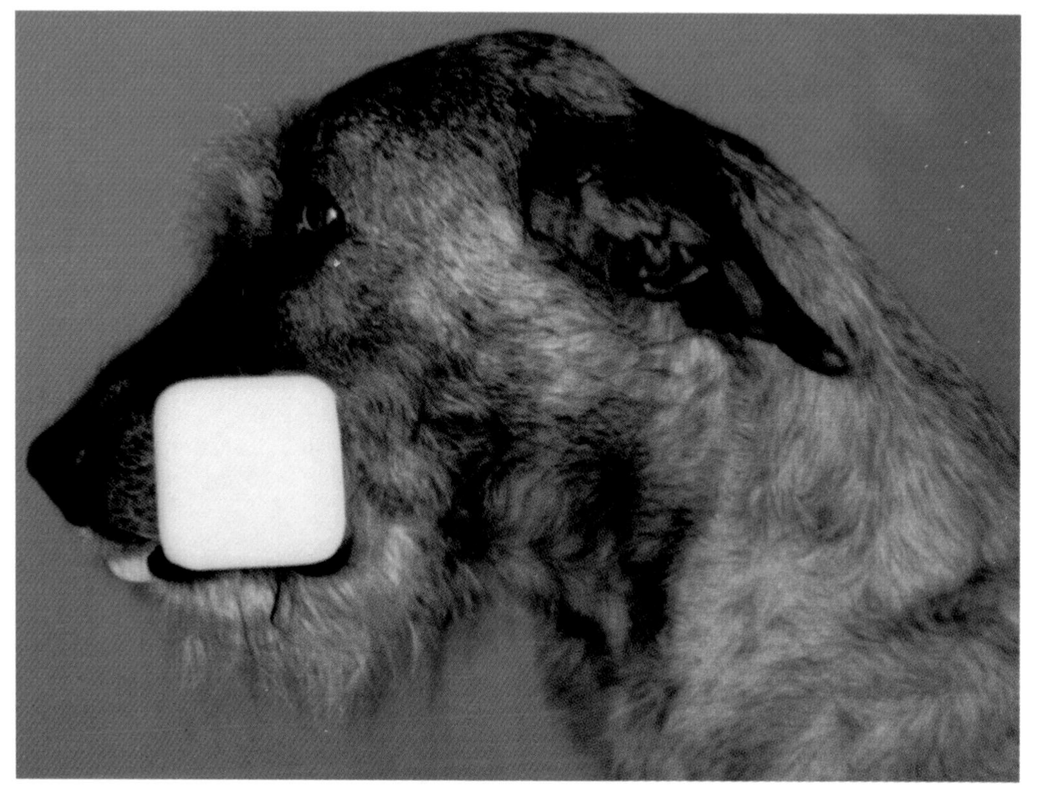

Dual Ch/OT Ch Superstar in Neon holds the dumbbell, demonstrating *Retrieve*.
Photo: Kevin Proud

Once you get through that, get down to the serious business of having fun again. Show your hound the dumbbell, and run. Hold it up high and let your hound jump for it if it wants to. Get your hound worked up and then throw the dumbbell for it. Make a big fuss over your dog for retrieving. Don't throw the dumbbell more than a couple of times. Wolfhounds are not natural retrievers and can become bored. They prefer to go after an object rather than bring it back.

It is important to understand that the purpose of training is not limited to obedience trial competition. Personal rewards are much greater than official scores. Many brilliant, well-trained Irish Wolfhounds never enter an obedience ring. Enjoy the learning experience together.

CHAPTER TWELVE

Norwegian Irish Wolfhounds in a natural setting.

THE IRISH WOLFHOUND WORLD-WIDE

Wolfhounds can be found in varying numbers throughout the world, including such places as Poland, Russia and Japan as well as in most of Scandinavia, the EEC, the Antipodes, South Africa and the United States of America and Canada. Several countries have sufficient numbers to have founded their own official Irish Wolfhound breed clubs under the governing body of the national kennel club, while others remain part of their country's official sighthound club.

Federation of European Irish Wolfhound Clubs

On the last weekend of April 1994, as part of the celebration of their 60th anniversary, the Irish Wolfhound Club of The Netherlands hosted an international gathering of delegates representing many clubs around the world. The purpose was to discuss the possible formation of a Federation in which participating countries would cooperate and exchange information, with the aim of promoting the interests of the breed and safeguarding its future. A steering committee undertook to prepare the groundwork and, in Dublin in July 1995, during the World Congress of Kennel Clubs, the Federation of European Irish Wolfhound Clubs (EIWC) was founded. A Board was elected and, in accordance with Article 19 of the Articles of Association, the President of the Irish Wolfhound Club of Ireland (as country of origin of the breed) was named President of the EIWC – an honorary, non-executive position with the right to attend meetings of the Ruling Council and of the Management Committee and to vote at such meetings. Delegates of member clubs form the Ruling Council, which governs the EIWC and has the power to elect the Management Committee responsible for preparing and executing the decisions of the Ruling Council. An Irish delegate is always a member of the Management Committee.

Articles 4 and 5 of the Federation state: *The Purpose of the EIWC shall be to bring together, within a single framework, the Irish Wolfhound clubs or associations from as many European countries as possible, to make joint efforts to promote and improve the breed, and to foster friendship among Irish Wolfhound enthusiasts throughout the world.*

They go on to state that these aims shall be pursued as follows:

a) cooperation at all levels to promote the Irish Wolfhound breed
b) universal recognition of the established Standard of the Irish Wolfhound Club of Ireland, uniform acceptance of this Standard worldwide
c) exchange of judges between members
d) regular exchange of opinions between members and between judges
e) preparation of guidelines and recommendations in order to improve and harmonise the breed throughout the world
f) regular analysis of the health situation of the breed, and setting of health improvement objectives and programmes
g) organisation of European Irish Wolfhound shows
h) award of EIWC prizes for special occasions

i) publication of periodic news sheets
j) other appropriate activities

Determination of the Breed is covered under article 8 as follows: *The Standard of the Irish Wolfhound deposited with the Fédération Cynologique International (FCI) at any given time (the Standard) shall be recognised by the members of the EIWC and its judges. The Standard shall be an integral part of these Articles of Association. Adjustments to the Standard to be accepted by the FCI is the exclusive right of the Irish Wolfhound Club of Ireland.*

Each country may have more than one EIWC member club. Each member must also be a member of its own country's national dog association, as recognised by the FCI.

Where the interests of the Irish Wolfhound breed are promoted by a club that represents other breeds also, this club may apply for EIWC membership.

Irish Wolfhound clubs outside Europe can be associate members without any voting rights.

If a club is dissolved, ceases to be a member of its own country's national dog association or has not paid its membership fee for two years, its membership will be terminated automatically.

Members may withdraw from the EIWC at the end of any year by submitting notice of withdrawal to the Secretary of the Management Committee at least three months in advance.

Any club that seriously harms the interests of the IEWC may be expelled by a decision of the Ruling Council taken in a meeting by a two thirds majority of the delegates present. The club in question shall be notified of the reasons for the proposed expulsion not less than 60 days before the decision is taken, to give the club an opportunity to justify itself before the meeting of the Ruling Council.

The EIWC is established on a non-profit basis. All positions and work involved are accepted on a voluntary basis. Its liability extends only to its own assets; individual liability on the part of members is excluded and the EIWC is not liable for the obligations incurred by members.

The EIWC recognises the autonomy of the members and will not interfere with their internal affairs, although it may be called upon to settle such disputes as may arise.

The seat of the EIWC is located in the respective place of residence of the Chairman of the Management Committee.

This is a shortened summary of the Articles of Association of the Federation of European Irish Wolfhound Clubs. More information and details of programmes of any events to be held can be obtained through any of the national Irish Wolfhound Clubs.

Some of the following résumés of the breed in a few countries are taken from reports given by breed representatives at the International Irish Wolfhound Weekend organised by the Dutch Club in 1994.

Belgium

Here there is no separate Irish Wolfhound Club, but in 1986 the Belgian Sighthound Club decided to subdivide for different breeds and the Irish Wolfhound and Deerhound sections came into being. Greyhounds were later added to this section. Irish Wolfhound history in Belgium is relatively recent, starting at the end of the 1960s with hounds imported from the English kennels of Erindale, Petasmead and Brabyns. Mrs Welters-Well, known for the Hof van Rieth kennel of Dachshunds, began breeding quality Wolfhounds from a bitch imported from the Irish kennel of Ballykelly. The kennel van de Dampoort acquired some good Royden hounds and also owned and had progeny from Outhwaite Trostan (bred by Mr and Mrs Baird) in partnership with Mr and Mrs De Ridder. At about this time Mr and Mrs Seymus started the kennel Of the Good Heath with hounds imported from Holland, Erindale in England and Italy, and they bred some important hounds and several champions. The successes of their home-bred Ch Miss Marple of the Good Heath gained them the accolade of Top Breeders in 1991. Despite this and other great successes, this kennel gave up breeding Irish Wolfhounds, and most of their stock went to found the kennel Of Kilmara. Recently imported into Belgian kennels from England are Eaglescrag, Marumac and Solstrand hounds. Mr Das' kennel Of Easy Runner started with Wolfhounds from Holland and has also brought in good Wolfhounds for showing and breeding from Killykeen kennel, Ireland.

Denmark

The Danish Irish Wolfhound Club was founded in 1986. Today there are about 130 members and approximately 500 Wolfhounds, some 75 puppies being registered each year. Wolfhounds have been in Denmark since the 1930s, but very few were bred until the late 1960s, when stock was imported from Norway, Sweden, England and Ireland and good hounds were bred by the Ragger and Ballydane kennels, among others. These kennels stopped breeding in the 1970s, but offspring from them founded kennels such as Ulvsholm, which later imported influential dogs from the USA and went on to produce several champions. Faxbo kennel also began around this time, and to date it has produced a great number of litters and about 12 champions. In 1993 the Top Winning Wolfhound in Denmark was Wolfhouse Georgia on my Mind, and this kennel has recently imported Ch Superstar in Command from Canada to add to the gene pool. From its foundation in 1981, the kennel Nadia-Blue owned by Nelly Jensen has been very successful, producing at least one champion per litter so far. Her original hounds came from Lene Bang-Pedersen, who produced many top winning Wolfhounds and much important breeding stock.

At the International Irish Wolfhound weekend held in the Netherlands in 1994, the Danish Club reported that the type and quality of their hounds has improved over the years, and that the hounds are sound, with few health problems.

Italy

Although Italy has no breed club, interest in Irish Wolfhounds is increasing here and there are now about 200 in the country. The Irish Wolfhound first came to Italy in 1956, when Countess Lulling Buschetti imported the six-month-old bitch, Sanctuary Rite. Two years later, a Sanctuary dog and a Sulhamstead bitch were imported as foundation stock for the Countess' Da Maser kennel. When Ch Sulhamstead Merman became the first Wolfhound to win Crufts, his brother Sulhamstead Marshal was purchased by the kennel. In 1967 a bitch was imported from Ballykelly, Ireland. However, the Da Maser kennel is not actively breeding or showing today.

The arrival in 1971 of an Eaglescrag bitch, who took four CACs and one CACIB in a year, awakened interest in the breed in Italy. In the same year the import of Blackdale Murdoch from Ireland founded the Del Solengo kennel, which quickly gained recognition when both Murdoch and a bitch from the Fionn Uisge kennel in Ireland won their international titles. In 1975 there were just 18 Irish Wolfhounds registered in Italy, and Antonio Salmon bought stock from Del Solengo and from Erindale (England) to found the Bassa Pavese kennel. This kennel went on to import many Wolfhounds from Ireland and England, and stock from here founded several new kennels such as Pugnale, Fergian and Vecchio Martello. From these kennels many hounds took national and international titles. By 1985 numbers had dropped, but hounds were imported from The Netherlands and Belgium and soon won their titles. Today there is an increasing demand for good Wolfhounds in Italy.

Norway

The Norwegian Wolfhound Club was founded in 1978 with a total of 75 members. Today, membership is around 280 and approximately 400 hounds are registered. Due to the geography of Norway, the Club divides its activities into several districts, with a contact person in each area to help, advise and organise social gatherings, lectures and ring-training classes. Four times a year an excellent and informative magazine is produced and a club championship show with a specialist judge is held in June or July.

This club takes very seriously the hereditary health problems within the breed and has set up screening and testing programmes. Longevity records show the current average lifespan of hounds in Norway to be seven to eight years.

Wolfhounds first came to Norway in the 1930s from the Ifold kennels, England, and the 1950s saw the arrival of Ballykelly and Boroughbury hounds. One of the earliest kennels was Kroodden, owned by Ulf Rosfjord, and progeny from this stock became influential in founding the Innsetlia kennel of Susanne Kleffelgard and the Wenwil kennel, which also had Mountebanks stock from Sweden. In 1974, Wenche and Kaare Stray brought in Marumac Amos from England and he quickly gained his international title. Several new kennels began in the 1980s and hounds were imported from Sweden, particularly from Westmount and Rovaleco kennels, and also from Marumac and Brabyns kennels in England, whilst Nickelodeon

A magnificent Irish Wolfhound in a rugged Norwegian landscape.
Photo: Sjur Giljane

Wolfhounds should be bred for an active, outdoor lifestyle.
Photo: Sjur Giljane

Harp of Eagle came from Sam Ewing in America. More recently, stock has been acquired from the Killykeen kennels, Ireland. Among several kennels currently showing with notable success are Cormac, Chess Art, McKenzie, O'Marksbay and Irski.

Sweden

The Swedish Irish Wolfhound Club was founded in 1976 as a sub-division of the Swedish Sighthound Club. Initially there were 30 members and 92 Wolfhounds were registered with the Norwegian Kennel Club, but by 1993 the membership had risen to over 550 and the number of hounds registered to 136. The club is not official, so has no show or championship status, although its policy is to have breed specialists from all over the world to judge at the shows it arranges. The club was founded with the purpose of fostering sound breeding policies and sharing knowledge about the care and training of the breed.

Almost all breeding stock in Sweden today can be traced back through the generations to just two kennels of the 1960s: the Mountebank kennel of Mrs Carin Lindhé and the Ljuna kennel of M and B Johansson. Mrs Lindhé brought in some very important and influential hounds at that time; Brackenford Ballinderry Patricia (winner of the Golden Dog Award in 1968) contributed much, as did Brackenford Moya, Donbeg Shannon and Driella of Eaglescrag, who was in pup to Branwen Luath. One of these puppies was the famous Mountebanks Barrabas, and he and Patricia both produced excellent hounds who formed the foundation of many new kennels. The Ljuna kennel imported Boroughbury males and a Brabyns bitch and their progeny was to prove influential. These kennels provided foundation stock for the Furlong kennel.

The 1970s saw the rise of several new kennels and hounds were imported from some of the top British kennels of the time as well as from Wild Isle, in America, to widen the gene pool in the Clansman kennel of U and U Högberg. The Wolf Tone kennels of E and L Janzon began with Eaglescrag hounds, and the Westmount Kennels of Eva and Jan Söderqvist mated their imported bitch, Buckhurst Guinevere, to Mountebanks Atticus, thus founding a line of important and influential stock. Later, Mochras and Solstrand hounds were imported and used by Westmount, the resultant progeny being used by both established and new kennels. E and S Wranéus began the Wild Eagle kennel with Petasmeade hounds from England. The popularity of the breed rose appreciably in the 1980s and more new kennels were registered and have been breeding and showing with varying degrees of success.

Switzerland

The Irish Wolfhound Club of Switzerland was founded in 1985 and now has about 166 members, owning about 200 hounds. Each year the Club has its own show and nominates judges for the annual national and international shows. A brief newsletter is published three times a year.

The first Wolfhounds were seen in Switzerland about 100 years ago, but nothing further is reported until well after the War, when an Ardkinglas male was imported. Only in the 1970s and 1980s did the breed become relatively popular, and there are now 10 active breeders (the Club regulating the breeding of Wolfhounds). The best-known breeding kennel is that of Mr and Mrs Erath, whose male Moloney of Green Island recently became an FCI World Champion.

Although the breed is numerically small, the quality of hounds bred here is good. Current life expectancy is between seven and eight years and there are few health problems.

Aus Ch Tirsilin Bronson.

The Netherlands

The Irish Wolfhound Club of The Netherlands was established in 1934. At first Wolfhounds were combined with Deerhounds, whose separate club was recognised in 1983. The stated objective of the Wolfhound Club is to unify breeders and ensure that healthy hounds of good temperament are being bred according to the breed standard and raised and trained correctly. The policy is to strive for as broad a breeding base as possible.

Aus Ch Cilldara Cormac.
Photo: Robin Twig

Until about 1960 there were only about 30 members. Then interest increased rapidly, with 250 members in 1970 and more than 600 today. Currently there are about 1200 Irish Wolfhounds in The Netherlands. The club organises a championship show as well as a show for young hounds and veterans. There are breeders' and new members' meetings as well as a get-together for lure coursing and a New Year walk.

Health in the breed is taken very seriously and, since 1983, on-going investigation into portosystemic shunt (liver shunt) has been undertaken by the University of Utrecht, working closely with the Club members. Their findings have been made available to all Wolfhound clubs. A priority of the club is to improve the lifespan of hounds, which is currently about eight years, and there is also a study group investigating heart-related problems.

With such conscientious owners and breeders, the standard of Irish Wolfhounds in The Netherlands today is very high, many judges reporting that this country has some of the best in the world today, with few problems of size or soundness.

Australia

(kindly contributed by Francis McEvoy of Tirowen Irish Wolfhounds)

Before the early 1970s there is little factual information about this breed in Australia, and yet dogs of Wolfhound type have gone into the folklore of the country. Those of us who were showing, particularly at country shows in the early 1970s during the re-introduction of the breed, well remember the numerous old bushmen who would come up, with the pleasure of recognition in their eyes, to share their memories of old 'staghounds' who 'looked just like that – and how they could hunt! But that was long ago, down on the river. We haven't seen any for ages.' And they would admire the size and bone of these new youngsters, and speculate on how they would fare in the bush.

To me, these experiences always recalled A Dawson's book *Finn the Wolfhound,* and his life free in the outback, not so far-fetched if you know the breed and the country. Readers may also be familiar with the description in *The Irish Wolfhound Club Yearbook 1935–1937* (Great Britain), cited also in early editions of *The Complete Irish Wolfhound* by Alma Starbuck, of Mr Monroe's Australian-bred dog, Thunder, and his hunting exploits with rabbit, kangaroo and deer. These stories may have seemed unrealistic or fanciful to those who did not know the real capabilities of this great hunter, but they are all too likely to those who have seen the hounds in the bush.

Several Irish Wolfhounds were imported in the 1920s, mostly for use on properties, but it should not be supposed that hunting was the only function of these hounds in those early days. The photograph from the early 1920s on page 182 shows they clearly had a rôle as housedogs for the gentry at the turn of the century; here we see Mrs Beck of Beaumont looking out from her home in the foothills overlooking Adelaide, with her companion, unmistakably a Wolfhound, at her side. Some Wolfhounds were also registered and shown with success in the 'between wars' period, and again in the mid-1950s. After this there appears to have been no registered stock left in the country.

The breed was re-introduced in the early 1970s and has developed almost exclusively from a small pool of imports brought in from Great Britain, with only a dash of the Irish! It would be fair to say that these 'pioneers' came from rather mixed sources and were of varying quality, a fact which reflected the limited contacts and differing motives of those first owners. For some, quite frankly, this was a 'new breed', of dramatic impact and high curiosity value, with significant financial possibilities. For others, it was a sentimental grasping of a cultural icon, a tangible link with the romance of Irish ancestry and the world of Celtic mystery and mythology. Whatever the reason, this was the origin of the breed in the 1970s in Australia, and the basis from which it has developed.

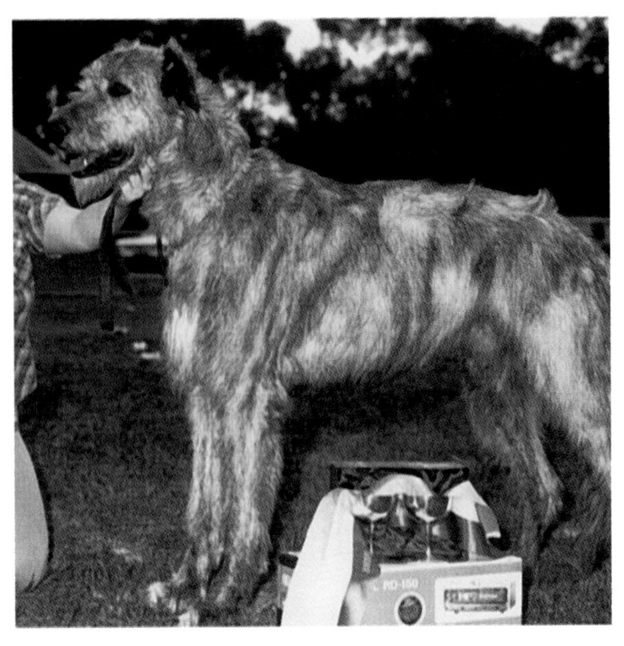

Aus Ch Erindale Trader Prince.
Courtesy of Kilrain kennel.

Amongst the early imports, those that stand out for their quality and their contribution to the positive development of the breed were: Fitztearlach Tamara (Pilelo kennels); Erindale Cathy (Ole kennels); Erindale Fortuna, Eaglescrag Tara Tirowen, Eaglescrag Kester Tirowen (Tirowen kennels); Eaglescrag Merinda (Glenmaer kennels); Erindale Trader Prince (Kilrain kennels); Royden Jasper and Drakesleat Krysten of Kilkaren (Kilkaren kennels). No doubt another observer would add to this list, but these kennels all imported their original stock, and have provided the starting point for many of the current owners and breeders in this country today, and they deserve to be remembered for their hard work and dedication.

The difficulties and disappointments faced by these early breeders are evident in the 'survival figures' from this original list, only the Tirowen and the Glenmaer kennels remaining active in the breed today. Since then, however, many have come to know and love the Wolfhound, and some of these newcomers have made their mark in producing strong and typical animals as worthy pets, companions and show dogs. Of these, Ramarego (Ms C Maciver, NSW) and Roscormac (Mr and Mrs Jeanes, Victoria) are probably foremost.

In the show ring, the premier shows for the breed are undoubtedly the three Specialties and the annual Royal Shows held in each state. The Irish Wolfhound Club of Victoria hosts one Specialty, usually in March/April each year in Melbourne, and the Irish Wolfhound Club of New South Wales conducts fixtures at Easter and again in October, both in Sydney. Average entry at these shows is between 40 and 50 dogs, some exhibitors travelling considerable distances to attend. This number contrasts with the entry at regular all-breed shows, which can descend to a single specimen; rarely does it exceed 10. The Royal Shows attract larger entries but, because they are typically held over 10 days, they present additional practical difficulties for interstate exhibitors. Entries here range from 20 to 30 in better years.

There are many all-breed shows, both at championship and open level, for those who wish to campaign their Wolfhounds in our climate (typically warm and dry). These can be very pleasant social days. To become an Australian Champion a dog must win a total of 100 challenge points in a minimum of four challenges under different judges. The points are determined by the number of Wolfhounds of the same sex beaten at the show. Over the years there have been many Australian champions, some excellent specimens of the breed, others perhaps not so good, but four go down in history as *firsts* of the re-introduction era: Aus Ch Erindale Cathy became the first Australian Champion in 1973; Aus Ch Tirowen Cilwych Mor was first to win a full Hound Group in 1978; Aus Ch Erindale Trader Prince was first to go all the way to BIS at an All-Breed

Aus Ch Eaglescrag Kester Tirowen. Photo: Barkleigh-Shute

Championship Show, which he did twice, in 1977 and 1978: and Aus Ch Wolftone Trean won the first Specialty at Easter 1979.

As was suggested earlier, quality in the breed here is rather erratic. Because of the limited number of imports over the years, it is generally not possible to talk clearly about 'lines' in Australia. Perhaps the most successful exception to this is the Tirowen kennel of Francis and Anne McEvoy. Based on Eaglescrag imports over a period of 25 years, this has resulted in a series of outstanding bitches, who have been at the forefront of the breed for almost two decades. Their first import, Aus Ch Eaglescrag Tara Tirowen, was BIS at the Irish Wolfhound Club of New South Wales in October 1980; her daughter Aus Ch Tirowen Katriona went Reserve BIS in 1985; her daughter Aus Ch Tirowen Jessica took BIS in 1986; the next two generations took BIS at the Irish Wolfhound Club of Victoria in 1993 and 1995; and Tirowen Carillon was Reserve BIS at New South Wales and BIS at Victoria in 1996 at less than two years old. This record is a tribute to the quality of stock sent to the McEvoys from Mr and Mrs Jenkins' Eaglescrag kennels and, more recently, from Mrs Kenis-Pordham in Great Britain.

The other difficulty faced by conscientious breeders is that most of the judges in Australia are 'generalists'. The numbers in any one breed are rarely sufficient to support a specialist judge. This has its good side in that the simple things like a correct bite and soundness, easy decision points on which a judge can focus, are now very strong here. It does not, however, mean that type or movement in the wider sense is good, because these people often do not understand the basic function and structure of our hound. The outline, with appropriate length of leg and body, is too easily lost to the more compact, generally smaller 'show type', lacking the true features of our breed. The other casualty to a degree has been in some of the finer points, such as eye colour, ear shape and size and coat texture. For a long time, too *of great size* was apparently translated as *fat* and we certainly struggled to hold the hound shape with its flowing and graceful lines, against the *blob*!

Until comparatively recently, new blood in the breed has meant importing, generally (because of Government Regulations) from Great Britain or Ireland. This is both difficult and expensive and it has not always been possible for the importers to choose a puppy personally, so they have had to rely on breeders to send them a good one. They have not always been well served in this, but much credit must go to the breeders overseas who did send quality stock, and to those far-sighted and committed individuals who took on the daunting risks. Fortunately the time in quarantine has now been reduced, so the list of countries from which we may import has increased.

Technology is becoming an increasingly viable option for breeders in this country, recognised and sanctioned by the local Kennel Controls. Already, at least three litters have been born as a result of using frozen semen from overseas: two from a Swedish sire, one from an American dog. Although still a high-risk, high-cost procedure, involving pin-point accuracy in timing and usually a surgical procedure for implantation, the prospects are exciting, holding out the possibility of some of the best breeding stock in the world being available to improve the breed in this country. If breeders take up this opportunity wisely, we could see Australia as the leader in the Irish Wolfhound world for the quality and genetic strength of this wonderful hound.

New Zealand

(kindly contributed by Jane Usmar of Ballyboughal Irish Wolfhounds)

New Zealand is a beautiful Pacific country of approximately 100,000 square miles, similar in size to Great Britain but with a population of only 3,500,000 people. We are mainly an agricultural nation, although increasingly tourism and manufacturing are becoming significant factors in the economy. Our climate is temperate; in Spring and Autumn the temperature would be much the same as in the South of Ireland. For this reason, the Wolfhound puppies who have been imported during these seasons experience no climatic shock, although it seems to take a couple of years for their coats to adapt to our 'back-to-front' seasons. There is no quarantine

NZ Ch Banrac Derrysheehan.

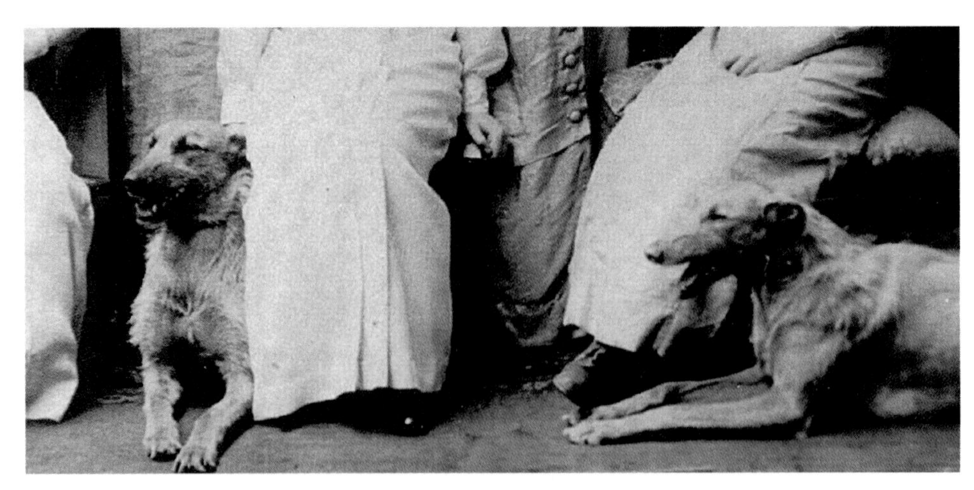

Photograph of Irish Wolfhounds in New Zealand, c 1900, from an early settler museum.
Courtesy of Erik Oostendorp.

... and an early Australian Wolfhound, photographed with Mrs Beck in the early 1920s.
Courtesy of the National Trust, Australia.

period for dogs coming in from Ireland, Great Britain or Australia, and our imports to date have been from these countries, from kennels such as Ballykelly, Nutstown, Brabyns, Eaglescrag, Clonara, Gulliagh, Ballalyn, Seplecur and, more recently, Chappeleigh, Bokra and Ainsea. With the easing of restrictions predicted from the USA and the willingness of the New Zealand Kennel Club to register puppies sired by artificial insemination, we will doubtless see new strains coming into the country. The current regulations permit the imports to be taken straight to their new home with no apparent stress factor, in spite of their 12,000 mile flight.

However, our small population is reflected in the breed numbers and, because of our isolation, we have a very limited gene pool. About 60 Irish Wolfhounds have been imported since Ballykelly Eoin first arrived in 1965 and at the moment only a handful of these owners are actively showing and breeding. Inevitably there appears to be a huge variation in breed type and no kennels are sufficiently established to stamp that definitive image which makes a particular kennel and line instantly recognisable.

The ever-increasing number of judges now visiting from all over the world has had considerable effect in raising the breed's profile and, with the confidence that comes from showing under a judge who has a working knowledge of the Standard, the future looks a lot brighter. Over recent years the Irish Wolfhound Club of New Zealand has been fortunate in obtaining the services of several overseas breed specialists for the annual championship shows, and their expertise and assistance has been invaluable. A growing interchange of puppies and ideas between Australia and New Zealand bodes well for trans-Tasman relationships.

It is gratifying to see good stock arriving here from recognised kennels, as the future of our home-bred dogs depends on Wolfhounds with good conformation and health. Seventy per cent of our club members are pet owners and, as care-takers of our wonderful breed, it behoves us to produce happy and healthy companion hounds as well as successful show stock.

United States of America

There is evidence to show that an Irish Wolfhound arrived in America with Christopher Columbus, having embarked with its young master when the ship docked at Galway to take on supplies and Irish crew. Father Hogan refers to the exportation of Irish Wolfdogs to America and in 1825 Major Strickland describes how Neptune, a *remarkably fine Irish greyhound*, tracked and caught a bear in Canada. Records also show that General Roger D Williams of Lexington, Kentucky was breeding Wolfhounds with stock that could be traced back to Dhulart and Sheelagh (recorded in Captain Graham's pedigree book). In 1897, his Ailbe and Moira were the first two Irish Wolfhounds to be registered with the America Kennel Club. In 1912 registrations increased when the Newry Hounds of Joseph A McAleenan were recorded and Mr Horace Hill imported hounds from the Felixtowe kennels, England and registered them under his Toyon affix.

Cragwood, one of the greatest American kennels, owned by Mrs Norwood B Smith, was founded on Toyon stock. Mrs Smith registered her first litter in June

1921. Three years later, Cragwood hounds formed the foundation of Mr and Mrs L O Starbuck's famous and very important Ambleside kennel.

Interest in the breed grew quickly, and more Wolfhounds were appearing at shows. This inspired Mrs Smith to start a breed club, and in 1927 The Irish Wolfhound Club of America was sanctioned by the American Kennel Club, with Mrs Norwood B Smith as President and Mr L Starbuck as Secretary / Treasurer.

Other important breeders at this time were Mr and Mrs Edward Clark, who owned the Halcyon kennel and had brought in top-class hounds from Great Britain and France, and Mr Charles Burrage of the Rathain Kennel. In 1928, Mr and Mrs Groverman Ellis started the great and influential Killybracken kennel. The early 1930s saw Mr and Mrs Haskell import some of the best of the Brabyns hounds from Captain Hudson into their Whippoorwill kennels. Meanwhile, Jeannette McGregor established the very important Kihone kennel, based on carefully chosen imported stock whose subsequent progeny were to prove invaluable to the future of the breed. These eminent kennels worked together, using one another's stud dogs and producing magnificent hounds of excellent type, size and quality, providing outstanding stock for others to capitalise upon.

The mid-1930s saw the arrival of Mr and Mrs Fess (Taraledge), who worked tirelessly for the breed and were resposible for originating and editing the club's official magazine, *Harp and Hound*. Another outstanding kennel was formed by Colonel and Mrs Wofford of the Rathrahilly affix; a little later Mrs Peter van Brunt moved the Riverlawn kennel to Lake Placid and became more active in the breed.

The Misses Dalton and Cram first registered their Hillaways affix in 1952, and their Am Ch Hillaways Padraic of Eagle, owned by Sam Ewing, proved a great winner and important stud dog, siring many champions. Despite being in the breed for a very short period, Mr Thomas Wanamaker was to have great success in the show ring and as a breeder with his Edgecliff hounds. He imported Tara of Ouborough from Great Britain and, mated to Am Ch Arnold of Edgecliff, she produced outstanding progeny at a time when top quality breeding stock was at a premium. One of the offspring, Am Ch Brian Boru of Edgecliff, won three Hound Groups, an unprecedented success at that time. Fortunately, Tara's puppies were bought by knowledgeable and appreciative breeders and went on to prove their individual worth as stud dogs and brood bitches.

The 1950s was a time of stability for the Wolfhound fraternity in America, quality hounds being bred by knowledgeable people with guidance from the founders of the breed. Interest in showing both at Specialty and all-breed shows was fostered, and regional clubs were founded for social and educational purposes. The first National Specialty Show ever held in the West was in 1951 at Long Beach, California, judged by Esther Croucher of the Rippingdon Kennels, Great Britain. She declared Rory of Kihone the perfect type to revitalise and improve the breed in Great Britain, and his owner, Miss McGregor, kindly sent him as a gift to British breeders. In 1956, Ch Tralee of Ambleside created a record, becoming the first Irish Wolfhound ever to win three Specialties. Newcomers to the breed quick to make their mark were Samuel E Ewing III, of the Eagle kennel, who is still enormously successful in the ring today, and General Alfred de Quoy of the Keltic affix who, until his recent death, worked tirelessly for the breed, promoting obedience work and writing several in-depth and erudite studies relating to Wolfhounds.

The following decades saw ever-increasing numbers of Irish Wolfhounds being bred and exhibited. Many new kennels came into being, some with more success than others, depending whether their owners were prepared to take advantage of and learn from the in-depth knowledge and experience of the 'elders' in the breed. As in all countries, too many novices went their own way, breeding indiscriminately, with a resultant divergence of type. Fortunately, in this vast continent there has always been a sufficient nucleus of truly knowledgeable and responsible breeders working to retain type and quality, so some American kennels can justifiably claim to produce some of the best Wolfhounds anywhere.

Prominent among the many top-class kennels of recent times were the Cu hounds of Mrs Kelly Fox, the Powerscourt kennels of Mrs Thomas Powers, the Major Acres hounds of Mary Major and the magnificent Fleetwind hounds bred by Mrs Lois Thomasson. Mr and Mrs Hall used well-bred hounds from Ireland in their Pequest Knoll kennel and Mrs Musson also used Ballykelly, Nendrum and Killykeen stock as a basis for the Maghera Glass kennel.

During the 1970s Mrs Jill Bregy set records in the show ring with her home-bred Am Ch Wild Isle Warlock, a dog greatly admired by top breeders and judges and a much-used and very influential sire. He won four National Specialties, his first at 14 months and his last from the Veteran class. He also won the Canadian Specialty three times.

Other affixes well-known for producing top-class hounds are:

Bailebrae	Maria Theresa Grotano
Fitzarran	Mr and Mrs Deemer (founded on Eaglescrag stock)
Lilliput	Mr and Mrs Little
Limerick	Janet and Linda Souza
Meadowbrook	Joel Samaha (greatly influenced by Mrs Nagle of Sulhamstead)
Singing Swords	Sue Engel

While there is still a great divergence in type and health problems are increasing among the large population of Wolfhounds in the United States of America, many dedicated, caring and truly knowledgeable breeders are upholding the ideals and standards of the great early kennels. Regional clubs and associations throughout the USA run shows and provide help, information and rescue services and the Irish Wolfhound Club of America still produces for its members the extremely informative and educational magazine *Harp and Hound.*

Sulhamstead Woodside in South Africa, 1973.

NZ Ch Ballyboughal Tir Eogain.

WHELPING CHART

Serve Jan:	1	2	3	4	5	6	7	8	9	10	11	12	13	14	15	16	17	18	19	20	21	22	23	24	25	26	27	28	29	30	31
Whelp Mar/Apr:	5	6	7	8	9	10	11	12	13	14	15	16	17	18	19	20	21	22	23	24	25	26	27	28	29	30	31	1	2	3	4
Serve Feb:	1	2	3	4	5	6	7	8	9	10	11	12	13	14	15	16	17	18	19	20	21	22	23	24	25	26	27	28	(29)		
Whelp Apr/May:	5	6	7	8	9	10	11	12	13	14	15	16	17	18	19	20	21	22	23	24	25	26	27	28	29	30	1	2	(3)		
Serve Mar:	1	2	3	4	5	6	7	8	9	10	11	12	13	14	15	16	17	18	19	20	21	22	23	24	25	26	27	28	29	30	31
Whelp May/Jun:	3*	4	5	6	7	8	9	10	11	12	13	14	15	16	17	18	19	20	21	22	23	24	25	26	27	28	29	30	31	1	2
Serve Apr:	1	2	3	4	5	6	7	8	9	10	11	12	13	14	15	16	17	18	19	20	21	22	23	24	25	26	27	28	29	30	
Whelp Jun/Jul:	3	4	5	6	7	8	9	10	11	12	13	14	15	16	17	18	19	20	21	22	23	24	25	26	27	28	29	30	1	2	
Serve May:	1	2	3	4	5	6	7	8	9	10	11	12	13	14	15	16	17	18	19	20	21	22	23	24	25	26	27	28	29	30	31
Whelp Jul/Aug:	3	4	5	6	7	8	9	10	11	12	13	14	15	16	17	18	19	20	21	22	23	24	25	26	27	28	29	30	31	1	2
Served Jun:	1	2	3	4	5	6	7	8	9	10	11	12	13	14	15	16	17	18	19	20	21	22	23	24	25	26	27	28	29	30	
Whelp Aug/Sep:	3	4	5	6	7	8	9	10	11	12	13	14	15	16	17	18	19	20	21	22	23	24	25	26	27	28	29	30	31	1	
Served Jul:	1	2	3	4	5	6	7	8	9	10	11	12	13	14	15	16	17	18	19	20	21	22	23	24	25	26	27	28	29	30	31
Whelp Sep/Oct:	2	3	4	5	6	7	8	9	10	11	12	13	14	15	16	17	18	19	20	21	22	23	24	25	26	27	28	29	30	1	2
Served Aug:	1	2	3	4	5	6	7	8	9	10	11	12	13	14	15	16	17	18	19	20	21	22	23	24	25	26	27	28	29	30	31
Whelp Oct/Nov:	3	4	5	6	7	8	9	10	11	12	13	14	15	16	17	18	19	20	21	22	23	24	25	26	27	28	29	30	31	1	2
Served Sep:	1	2	3	4	5	6	7	8	9	10	11	12	13	14	15	16	17	18	19	20	21	22	23	24	25	26	27	28	29	30	
Whelp Nov/Dec:	3	4	5	6	7	8	9	10	11	12	13	14	15	16	17	18	19	20	21	22	23	24	25	26	27	28	29	30	1	2	
Served Oct:	1	2	3	4	5	6	7	8	9	10	11	12	13	14	15	16	17	18	19	20	21	22	23	24	25	26	27	28	29	30	31
Whelp Dec/Jan:	3	4	5	6	7	8	9	10	11	12	13	14	15	16	17	18	19	20	21	22	23	24	25	26	27	28	29	30	31	1	2
Served Nov:	1	2	3	4	5	6	7	8	9	10	11	12	13	14	15	16	17	18	19	20	21	22	23	24	25	26	27	28	29	30	
Whelp Jan/Feb:	3	4	5	6	7	8	9	10	11	12	13	14	15	16	17	18	19	20	21	22	23	24	25	26	27	28	29	30	31	1	
Served Dec:	1	2	3	4	5	6	7	8	9	10	11	12	13	14	15	16	17	18	19	20	21	22	23	24	25	26	27	28	29	30	31
Whelp Feb/Mar:	2	3	4	5	6	7	8	9	10	11	12	13	14	15	16	17	18	19	20	21	22	23	24	25	26	27	28	1*	2	3	4

• Adjust for leap year.

BIBLIOGRAPHY

Books I used as reference sources for the history and development of the breed

Gardner, Phyllis *The Irish Wolfhound: a Short Historical Sketch* Dundalk, 1931
A scholarly and in-depth book of the history of the Irish Wolfhound, from earliest records in the 1920s. Illustrated with prints of wood engravings made by the author and her sister.
Graham, *Capt* George Augustus *The Irish Wolfhound* Dursley, 1879
Hogan, *Father* Edmund S J *The Irish Wolfdog* Dublin, 1897
Squire, Charles *Celtic Myth and Legend: Poetry and Romance* Newcastle Pub Co, 1975

Note: these books are out of print and difficult to obtain.

Further breed books

Gordon, John *The Irish Wolfhound*
Hudson, D E S *The Brabyns Handbook on Irish Wolfhounds*
Illustrated with the author's own excellent drawings of important and interesting hounds.
Hudson, Susanne *Gelert, that Peerless Hound*
Murphy, Elizabeth C *Raising, Showing and Breeding the Irish Wolfhound*
The revised edition of a very popular and informative book, full of photographs and drawings.
Murphy, Elizabeth C *The Irish Wolfhound*
A collection of photographs and pedigrees of English and Irish hounds 1950-1990. A wonderful reference book.
Killykeen-Doyle, Anthony *A Discussion of the Irish Wolfhound*
A limited edition, hand-bound soft-cover book, beautifully printed and illustrated with many archival photographs from private collections and never previously published. Available only direct from the author.
Samaha, Joel *The New Compete Irish Wolfhound*
An update of Alma Starbuck's definitive book on the breed published in the United States in 1963. Joel Samaha brings the story of the Irish Wolfhound in the United States of America up to the 1990s.
Sutton, Catherine G *The Irish Wolfhound*
Quoy, Alfred W de *The Irish Wolfhound Guide*
A reference book of extensive factual data encompassing all things Wolfhound. For the serious student rather than those seeking generalised information.
Quoy, Alfred W de *The Irish Wolfhound in Competition*
A most interesting reference book for the statistically minded.

General

Cunliffe, Juliette *Popular Sighthounds*
A very good chapter on Irish Wolfhounds, and it is most interesting and helpful in understanding the breed to compare it with the other sighthounds and how they have evolved for a specific purpose.
Donovan, John *Gaelic Names for Celtic Dogs*
A fun little book to help with naming hounds and pronouncing Irish words.
Redlich, Anna *The Dogs of Ireland*
A relatively brief but most interesting history of each of the nine Irish native breeds.

INDEX